To Terry and Margaret,

from Iain and Charlotte

in fellowship in the gospel.

Colossians 2:2. 22nd September 1988.

'BASH'
A Study in Spiritual Power

edited by
John Eddison

Marshalls

Marshalls Paperbacks
3 Beggarwood Lane,
Basingstoke,
Hants, UK.

First Published by Marshall Morgan & Scott 1983

ISBN: 0 551 01057 6

Typeset in Linotron Garamond by Coats Dataprint, Smithton, Inverness.
Printed in Great Britain by Richard Clay (The Chaucer Press) Ltd,
Bungay, Suffolk

Contents

Introduction

Charles Hewitson Nash was forty years old when he married Frances Ferrier-Rowe, some sixteen years his junior, in St Matthew's Church, Croydon on 3rd October, 1893. The ceremony was performed by the Rev'd Thomas Causton whose son, nearly twenty-five years later, became my godfather. Charles Nash at this time was Vicar of St Mary's Church, Maidenhead, and it was there, on 22nd April, 1898, that his second son was born, and two months later christened Eric John Hewitson.

Bash always disliked the name 'Eric'. Perhaps it was still too reminiscent of Dean Farrer's famous book, but although it is not known how or when his nick-name first arose, it was always as 'Bash' that he was universally and affectionately known. He not only accepted this soubriquet, but welcomed it, which may seem surprising when we remember how he would never allow a nick-name to be given to a boy at his camps for fear of hurting sensitive feelings. But it was as 'Bash' that he liked to be known by his friends, and it is as 'Bash' that he will be referred to in this book.

Little is known about his boyhood. He was educated at Maidenhead College, an Independent Day School for Boys. His career there does not appear to have been particularly distinguished, though he received a few minor prizes, and I have in my possession a beautifully bound volume of the works of William Cowper, presented to him at the age of ten for 'Conduct', and still in its pristine condition.

After leaving school, he started work with an insurance firm in London and it was in 1917, on his way home to Maidenhead by train, that he finally faced and responded to the claims of Christ upon his life. It is not known how soon after this great turning-point he began to think of Ordination; and certainly for some little time he continued his work in the city, while at the same time helping with the work at St Mary's Church, and taking an active part in the Scout Movement attached to it.

Then in 1922, encouraged by the Bishop of London, Dr Winnington-Ingram, and supported by grants at his disposal, Bash went up to Trinity College, Cambridge, and then proceeded to Ridley Hall. He was made Deacon in 1927, and after serving two curacies, at St John's, Ealing and Emmanuel, Wimbledon, and a period as Chaplain at Wrekin College, Shropshire, he joined the Staff of the Scripture Union in 1932, and his real life's work began.

He remained on the Staff of Scripture Union until 1965, but continued a very active and fruitful ministry until he was eighty. It was then that his health began to fail, slowly at first and then more rapidly, and he died peacefully in his own home, the house where he had lived for over fifty years, on Sunday 4th April, 1982, just a few days before his eighty-fourth birthday.

Sir Winston Churchill (for whom Bash had an undying admiration) once remarked that it was often the people who had impressed him least who had influenced him most. Perhaps he was thinking of the Christian Nanny (Mrs Everest) of whom he had been so fond; but I remember relating this comment when I first heard it instinctively to Bash. There was nothing particularly impressive about him. He did not possess any of those qualities which normally appeal to boys. He was neither athletic nor adventurous. He claimed no academic prowess or artistic talent. It is true that he possessed certain gifts which would have been useful in any field – a remarkable intuition, a shrewd common sense, a degree of business acumen and a sense of humour. But the secret of his remarkable influence lay deeper than this.

There was an amazing sympathy about him, so that people felt that to him as to no one else they could 'unlock the heart and let it speak', knowing that he would appear to be neither shocked nor surprised by their confidences. There was also a unique gift for making the Christian message both understandable and attractive. And there was supremely a spiritual magnetism which sprang from his complete and unreserved dedication to Christ.

Perhaps the effect of his ministry can best be summed up in words that were written about him at the time of his death in the Church and the National Press:

> 'Bash . . . was a quiet, unassuming clergyman who never sought the lime-light, hit the head lines or wanted preferment; and yet whose influence within the Church of England during the last

> fifty years was probably greater than any of his contemporaries, for there must be hundreds of men today, many in positions of responsibility, who thank God for him, because it was through his ministry that they were led to a Christian commitment.
>
> 'Those who knew him well, and those who worked with him, never expect to see his like again; for rarely can anyone have meant so much to so many as this quietly-spoken, modest and deeply spiritual man.'

It seems that just once in a while someone is raised up by God of whom his contemporaries say with complete sincerity, 'We shall never see his like again'; and that is what those of us who knew him found ourselves saying to each other when we heard that Bash had died. He was unique, but his influence will continue to be felt, not only in the work he created and nurtured, but in the hearts of that innumerable company of people who can say today, 'If it hadn't been for that man, I might have made a shipwreck of my life.'

* * *

What follows is not a biography, but rather a series of portraits, each painted from a slightly different standpoint, as the titles of the chapters suggest; but I have deliberately encouraged the writers to feel that their briefs extend beyond the title they have been given, so that they can describe the man they remember, and the personal impact he made upon their lives. Inevitably this has resulted in a certain amount of overlapping, repetition and even perhaps contradiction; but I have not felt it my duty as Editor to try to eliminate this defect, but as far as possible have left each portrait untouched, and thus sought to preserve the integrity of the work as a whole.

Crowborough
East Sussex
December, 1982

John Eddison

1: The man we knew

John Eddison

After a curacy in Tunbridge Wells, John Eddison joined the Staff of Scripture Union in 1942, and retired in 1980. For most of this time he was a colleague of Bash, and helped him at the camps at Iwerne Minster. He also ran the junior camps for preparatory schoolboys at Swanage. He is a governor of a number of independent schools, and has also written several books on the Christian life.

1: The man we knew

(This chapter is mainly a transcript of the sermon preached at Bash's Memorial Service in All Souls, Langham Place).

'Do you not know that there is a prince and a great man fallen in Israel this day?' (2 Samuel 3.38).

It is as a prince among spiritual leaders that those of us who knew him will always think of Bash, and as a great man that he will be remembered. I have often tried to analyse the texture of his greatness, and the secret of his far-reaching influence. Ultimately, of course, it lay in his whole-hearted and single-minded devotion to Christ, and his determination to put him first at all times and at any cost; but I think it is possible to discern a number of qualities which, under God, contributed to his remarkable power as a speaker, a counsellor and a friend.

It seems to me that greatness often consists in the harmony of opposites. In this respect it is rather like beauty. The beauty of a sunset, for example, consists in the daring and unpredictable way in which nature throws together colours which we would never dream of trying to combine in the decoration of a drawing-room. The beauty lies not in a compromise between opposites, but in their collision.

In the same way, if you study the life of any great man, and Bash was no exception, you will find it composed of a number of apparent contradictions or paradoxes. First among these I would mention his unusual combination of the spiritual and the natural. Most of us tend to live on two levels, and when, for example, the conversation takes a spiritual turn, there is usually some grinding of gears, the almost unconscious donning of an invisible cassock or phylactery. But this was not so with Bash. The two ran into each other. The transmission was automatic.

It was said of St Augustine that all his deepest thinking took the form of a conversation with God, and this was certainly what you felt about Bash. Prayer was the very breath of his life. He 'prayed without ceasing', for like a man with an 'incessant cough', he could not prevent himself at any moment from breaking out into prayer.

I remember how this was brought home to me on one of the last visits I paid him. His conversation had been rambling and uncertain. Even the beloved cucumber sandwiches seemed to be under some sort of a cloud, and were accused of backsliding. And then he prayed, and immediately twenty years fell away, and everything made sense. He was never more natural than when he was spiritual; and vice versa. A prayer would break quite naturally out of his conversation; and likewise a time of prayer might be punctuated with alarming and unexpected observations.

This could be embarrassing. If someone, in his view, went on praying for too long at a prayer meeting, then a neatly aimed 'Amen' would leave the performer hopelessly stranded in the middle of the pitch; while a quietly-spoken or more distant colleague would be told in a hoarse whisper to 'Speak up'. In anyone else such behaviour would have been reprehensible; but not with Bash, because his life was not departmentalised into a spiritual and a natural side. They permeated and infected each other.

I would frequently go into his room at camp and find him lying supine on his bed. It was difficult to tell whether he was praying or sleeping; but of this you could be quite sure: it was one or the other.

Again, he combined a love of tradition with a readiness for change. He did love the things of yesterday. He loved yesterday's bread. He loved yesterday's jokes. He took an almost childlike pleasure in hearing the same stories over and over again. It may have been when a group of us were having supper together at the end of a camp, that he would turn to me and say, 'Give us Duggie'; and to the groans of those who had heard it all before, I would be required to relate one of Douglas Argyle's legendary encounters with the Principal of Ridley Hall. Or it might be, 'Let's have Raven', and he would want to hear for the umpteenth time the story of that learned professor sheltering from a thunderstorm.

Yes, he loved the old. He loved the old hymns, like those chosen for his Memorial Service. He loved the old version of the Bible and the Prayer Book; and I tremble to think what he would have made of the 'ASB'. To the end he was what I would call a 'Thee and thou man'.

But at the same time he was prepared for change, and during the forty years or so in which he ran his camps, he adapted himself with conspicuous skill to changing circumstances: to the problems created by the war and to the period of reaction that followed it. He was not himself an initiator. Indeed, his initial reaction to suggested changes was always one of caution and even suspicion. He would not allow new ideas to pass unchallenged, and long and exhausting were the battles we sometimes had to convince him of the need for change. But it was a salutary exercise, for it made us think things through carefully and prepare our case; and once he was convinced he would quickly become reconciled, readily adapt himself, and rarely if ever want to put the clock back.

And then, once again, like his great hero, the Apostle Paul, Bash was both an idealist and a realist. He always knew exactly what he wanted, but he also knew what it was reasonable and practical to expect. If no great principle was at stake, he would bow to the wind rather than cause unnecessary offence. Now and then, for example, (sometimes perhaps with a little persuasion) 'the ox would fall into the pit', as he liked to put it, and his very strong views about Sunday would be relaxed.

In his counselling too, he would never expect too much too soon, and he often quoted the words of Jesus, 'I have yet many things to say to you, but you cannot bear them now'. As a matter of principle he rarely if ever went to a film or a play, but there was an occasion when a friend remembers being smartly kicked under the table because Bash thought he was on the point of making a derogatory remark about the theatre in the presence of a younger and less mature Christian.

He was at heart a pacifist, but he saw no point in preaching that doctrine to unregenerate men and women, because he realized that in the last resort war was probably the only way they had of settling their disputes; and for this reason accepted the need for a nuclear deterrent.

His belief in heaven was unshakeable, but unlike St Paul, he was in no hurry to get there. He loved life, and besides, he might have said with Nehemiah, 'I am doing a great work, so that I cannot come

– yet'. 'After all,' he said to me once, 'we are going to be dead for a very long time'.

No doubt those who felt that Paul was at times inconsistent would have felt the same about Bash. But he would have been justified in replying in the celebrated words of Emerson, that 'a foolish consistency is the hobgoblin of little minds'. Truth for Bash was certainly not a moving target, but, as Sir Winston Churchill said, 'the only way a man can remain consistent amid changing circumstances is to change with them, while preserving the same dominating purpose'.

And then again in Bash we had a man of great authority and yet great humility. It is not often that the wolf and the lamb, authority and humility, can be trained to lie down together, but they did so with Bash. It was because he spoke from his deep knowledge of the Bible, from the closeness of his walk with the Lord and from his own experience that his talks and his advice always carried such tremendous weight.

Mind you, there were times when this was not to our liking. Some of his letters, with their underlinings and their exclamation marks (the latter I sometimes felt being a rather unsuccessful attempt to dilute the effect of the former) needed a good deal of grace to receive. But I always admired his moral courage. He would stand by his principles and speak his mind, even if he knew that by doing so he might cause pain or incur misunderstanding.

I only once remember his courage failing him. He came up to Cambridge, so he said, to rebuke one of his camp officers who in a mild and undergraduate fashion had incurred his displeasure. I met him after the interview and asked him how he had got on. 'Oh', he said, 'he was so nice, and he gave me such a good breakfast, that I couldn't say anything'. He retreated to Maidenhead without firing a shot. But he need not have worried, for his intended target that day went on to become a diocesan bishop.

But I think that story also illustrates his humility. I suspect that most of us would have found some excuse for our silence which would have preserved our sense of self respect – 'I didn't think the time was quite ripe to speak', or 'I detected signs of penitence and so I remained silent.' But Bash was I think the most humble person I have ever known. He was prepared to look a fool for the sake of Christ. He always preferred the shadows to the limelight, and the foot-notes to the headlines; but if Balleine's 'History of the

Evangelical Party' were ever re-written to include the last fifty years, there would hardly be a page on which Bash would not figure in one of these.

Another mark of his humility was his willingness to delegate. In the early days of camp particularly, he gave some of us much more responsibility than we were really ready to assume; and although he was without peer as a speaker to boys, he rarely gave more than two talks at any one camp.

And I always admired too the way in which he accepted criticism, much of which was unjustified; for there is surely no greater test of humility that to see how it bears the imputation of undeserved blame. But Bash never harboured a grudge, and was always able to distinguish between the 'political' and the 'personal' – that is to say, he could disagree sharply with someone without making him an enemy. This is a distinction none of us finds easy, but it was a notable feature of Bash's character.

Perhaps nowhere was this combination of authority and humility seen to better advantage than in the way he chaired his officers' meetings every morning at camp. Although he was some fifteen to twenty years older than anyone else, he would encourage everyone to take part. Lively and protracted debates often followed, but gradually his authority would emerge, and with a gentle firmness, he would bring the discussion to an end, reaching,more likely than not, the conclusion he had wanted in the first place. I remember Henry Chadwick, for some years the director of music at the camps, comparing Bash's gentle dominance with the way in which the piano, in Beethoven's Fourth Piano Concerto, having given the orchestra plenty of time to have its say, quietly subdues it and stamps it with its authority.

I would like to mention next what I will call Bash's depth and simplicity. He knew his Bible better than most. He had a remarkable grasp of Christian doctrine and truth; and yet to hear him speak, there was scarcely a word which a child could fail to understand. He illustrated the truth of the saying that 'what a man is going to explain simply he must understand deeply'. I think this was one reason why his talks commanded such interest, and why he could rivet the attention of a lively and high-spirited audience of teenagers. Not until he was well into his seventies did he lose this astonishing grip, and he exploded for ever the belief that it is only the comparatively young who can speak to the very young.

Another paradox. He was industrious, and yet at the same time always relaxed. There was never a time when he was not, so to say, on parade or in action. I never remember his taking a proper holiday. Foreign travel made no appeal to him and he never went in an aeroplane. From time to time he would allow himself a few days at Eastbourne or Worthing, in Wales or the Lake District, but he was always accompanied by people whom he wanted to encourage or help, by his endless correspondence and by his inescapable prayer lists.

He had few hobbies. As a young man I believe he enjoyed playing chess, and he derived much pleasure from watching football and even boxing. He always said he enjoyed gardening, but at any rate latterly this seemed to consist mainly in supervising the efforts of young friends on his behalf, who were then suitably rewarded with Fuller's cake and cucumber sandwiches.

But although he was never off duty, it would have been difficult to find a more relaxed person. He always seemed at leisure, he was never in a hurry, and never too busy to laugh at a good joke, enjoy a new story, or join you for a meal.

Whatever we may think of his particular life-style, it seemed to suit Bash well enough. Indeed, it may have been the perfect recipe for old age, for he was active and energetic for many years after his retirement, and he was over eighty before he gave up regular speaking. He did not make the mistake which so many are tempted to make, of fore-spending his old age by over working as a younger man. His thermostat was set at just the right level. It cut out at about ten o'clock every night, by which time he liked to be in bed. It protected him from fruitless late-night discussions. It insulated him from intensity.

How he disliked intensity! I still have a picture in my mind of an occasion at some Conference, just before or after the war, when some soul-quaking talk had sent us all back to our rooms to think through what we had heard, on our knees. Somehow it was very comforting to learn that Bash had been found, propped up in bed, and reading 'Punch'.

I have said that he avoided overwork, and I think he did; but we must not forget two things. First, there was 'the care of all the churches' which came upon him daily, and from which he never sought release; and secondly, he never accepted the idea of retirement. The one thing that used to make him almost angry was to be asked about his retirement – when it would be or what it was like now it had come. 'Clergy don't retire', was his short, sharp retort.

Nor did he. And even during the last two or three years, when his strength was failing, and when he was so devotedly cared for by Dr. Mary McIver and others, the welfare of his beloved Iwerne Minster was never absent from his mind; and when that mind began to wander, it would wander into the library at Iwerne Minster, or to some other meeting which he was expecting to attend.

Another thing which always struck us about Bash was his almost equal enjoyment of society and solitude. He was the most companionable of men, and was always happy when friends could join him for a meal, or on a journey, or for a few days in the country or at the seaside. How often as under-graduates we used to linger with him far longer than we ought to have done, over breakfast, coffee or luncheon! 'But I've got a lecture, Bash; I must go now', we would protest. 'Cut it, man', would be the tempting reply; for there always seemed to be something interesting or important that he wanted to talk about.

And yet while this was true, a great deal of his time had perforce to be spent alone, and he genuinely seemed to enjoy his own company – thinking, praying, meditating, reading or planning; and quite often he would come out with a remark on some subject which showed how much more widely his mind had ranged over it than we might had supposed.

He seemed to possess all those inner resources which are essential for Christian living, and perhaps especially so for someone like himself who had deliberately chosen the single life. He would frequently seek the advice of his friends about his health, his car, his financial affairs and even his clothing and food; but he would rarely if ever speak about those deeper moral and spiritual problems and conflicts which even he cannot have escaped. That inner self which for praise or sympathy is in many men so clamant, and in all more or less perceptible, was seldom glimpsed; and he never seemed to carry a wound, however slight, which needed human fingers for its healing.

I come to the last of these paradoxes, as I have called them, which I want to mention. I don't think I have ever met anyone with a greater desire for self-preservation and yet at the same time a greater willingness for self-sacrifice. His sense of humour just preserved him from hypochondria, but only just, for he took immense care of himself. He was deeply suspicious of the food he was required to eat away from home, and I can still see him at a Scripture Union Conference, sitting at his chest of drawers, and quietly consuming a rice pudding and some stewed cherries which he had taken the precaution of bringing with him in a suit case. There was always the latest panacea which he had discovered for all his ills, real or imaginary; and his doctors were chosen, we felt, less for their professional skill than for the extent to which their diagnoses were likely to coincide with his own.

He had a horror of 'pips' and 'bugs'. He loved tomatoes, but I cannot think why. He would discard the skin, then painstakingly remove all the pips, and finally try to manœuvre what was left – a shapeless blob of protoplasm – on to his fork. He thought pips of any sort might cause appendicitis, but he was not amused when I suggested that if he had his appendix removed he would be able to enjoy a lot of things he was at present denying himself. He dreaded surgery, which made it all the more remarkable that he should undergo two quite nasty operations calmly and cheerfully when he was well into his seventies.

Bugs were an even greater enemy than pips, and in his view seemed to possess magical qualities. The story is told that he received a telegram from someone to say that because he had developed mumps they could not meet as they had arranged to do. 'What did you do?' Bash was asked. 'Oh,' he replied, 'I burned the telegram and gargled.'

I sometimes wondered whether all this wasn't partly a pose, for we teased him unmercifully about it, and he never seemed to mind, and in fact rather enjoyed the mockery. Be that as it may, it certainly seemed to pay off in the end; for in the forty years or so for which he ran his camps, he never missed even part of one through illness, though there were occasions when he reigned from his bed.

But alongside this was his remarkable self-sacrifice. I have never met anyone who was more willing to devote his time and energy to the service of Christ, or to be so completely at the disposal of others. And it was not easy, the work he pioneered. He was trying to do in the schools what John Wesley two hundred years ago tried to do in the parishes, and he met, albeit in a politer form, with the same sort of misunderstanding, suspicion and hostility. It used to be said that 'public school religion is that which fits you for life and ruins you for eternity'. I believe there was some truth in that fifty years ago. I don't believe it is any longer true today, and I attribute this completely different climate very largely to the influence of Bash. '*Si monumentum requiris, circumspice*'.

For a sensitive, shy person like Bash, this kind of work called for great moral courage and self-sacrifice. It is not generally known, for example, how seriously he thought of marriage before the war, discarding the idea because he felt that it would restrict and curtail his freedom as a pioneer missionary. And make no mistake, that is precisely what he was, just as truly as if he had been called to work in India, Africa or Latin America.

But were there no warts on this remarkable, this unique man? Well, yes, I suppose there were. He was not always the easiest person to work with. There were times when he could be tiresome, even exasperating. But looking back, I am inclined to think that most of what we were tempted to describe as faults were more often than not the obverse side of his virtues.

As a young man, for instance, he was notoriously unpunctual. On one occasion he was due to be taking a funeral at St John's, Ealing. The cortège arrived at the door, but there was no sign of Bash. In desperation the verger found Bash's robes, and rushed down the street to meet him coming from his digs. As they made their way back to the church, the verger assisted him to divest himself of his coat, and put his robes on him. It was not altogether surprising that he earned the soubriquet, 'the late Mr Nash'.

But lapses of this sort were largely due to his total commitment to what he happened to be doing at the time. He would become so involved, that he would forget that someone might be anxiously awaiting him ten miles away; and it is only fair to add, and a tribute to his innate self-discipline, that this particular shortcoming was almost completely eliminated as he grew older.

He could be difficult to reason with, and logic was never his strong point. There was an occasion about thirty years ago when he, Philip Thompson (at that time the camp Secretary) and I met in London to discuss plans. Bash was worried because although increasing numbers of boys were coming to one or other of the two summer camps, too many in his view were coming for only part of the time, thus disrupting the programme and more importantly the syllabus of talks. Our suggestion was that instead of two almost over-crowded fortnightly camps we should have three of ten days each, because this, we argued, would reduce the number of part-timers. But try as we would we could not convince Bash that this would be so. Finally we pointed out that if we had twenty-eight camps of one day each we would eliminate the problem altogether, and working back from this *reductio ad absurdem* we were at last able to convince him of the value of our proposal. Whether he really could not understand, or was simply fighting (as he was wont to do) a stubborn rear-guard action against a dangerous experiment, we shall never know. Suffice it to say that he never looked back or questioned the decision, and that pattern, adopted in the early 1950's, has continued to this day; and it would not surprise me if Bash credited himself with the inspiration for the change.

But I think we all felt that for him to dispense with logic was perfectly permissible, because his almost feminine intuition was so uncannily accurate, and the trouble only began when he tried to rationalise what he felt instinctively to be the right course of action. There was an occasion when he wrote to Mark Ruston and said, 'I feel we ought to get officers to camp a day earlier, and I have written to John Eddison for three good reasons'.

I think at times he was inclined to be a little ruthless, even intolerant, and did not disguise his irritation and impatience at foolish answers and inane laughter. And yet once more I feel that this was merely the reflection of deeply held convictions and ideals; and in any case, is not a streak of hardness an almost essential ingredient in the character of any good leader?

I suppose his enemies might have accused him on occasion of being disingenuous; but it was his determination to do his Master's will at almost any cost which led him now and then to bend the rules or to cut corners. He was too at times a little prone to exaggeration; but this was merely the overflow of his enthusiasm.

No, I don't think of these things as serious warts, but rather as freckles – almost endearing features, which reminded us that this prince of spiritual leaders was a man with passions like our own, and which threw into even sharper relief his many outstanding virtues.

But there was one criticism of Bash which I feel was unjustly levelled. It concerns his attitude towards women. It is true that with younger women, until he got to know them, he was reserved and defensive; but in the company of older women he quickly thawed, and became warm and expansive. It is true that his advice to young men about marriage was cautious and restrained. He never regarded it, as some do, as an inherent right which every Christian can claim. He did not hesitate to point out its hidden problems as well as admitting its obvious delights. This policy did expose him to a certain amount of obloquy, but it was marvellously vindicated by results, if we may judge by the extremely high percentage of happy and successful marriages made by his followers.

It is true that he was a shy man, without very much in the way of small talk; and it is true again, as every clergyman has found, when preoccupied with other thoughts, that at times he failed to remember a name or a face, and this may have caused an offence he never intended. But all of us who had him to stay in our homes were invariably struck by his unfailing courtesy, his irresistible charm, his perfect manners and consideration. This I know is what struck my own mother. Before the war we used to run drawing-room 'squashes', to which a number of well known people came to speak. I can still remember an occasion on which we were discussing possible speakers. Various high-powered performers were suggested, and then my mother said, 'Let's have Bash again. He's such a gentleman'. And if we may adopt his own definition of a Gentleman – 'someone with the strength of a man and the gentleness of a woman' – that is exactly what he was.

I first met Bash in the summer of 1932. I was at a house party in the Isle of Wight. It was a Sunday evening, about six o'clock, and I can see myself now sitting and reading alone. I had an inner feeling of discontent, because I did not seem to share what so many around me – officers and boys – so obviously appeared to possess, an inner joy and radiance.

It was at this moment that Bash came into the room, and seeing me alone, asked me if I would like to have a talk. I followed him into his room and we sat down and talked. I cannot now remember a single word he said, but I do know that I came out of that room a different person. Something had happened. It was as if a limb which had long been dislocated had suddenly clicked back into place; and I look back on that summer evening, 21st August 1932, as the great turning point in my life; and I have no doubt that if those present at Bash's memorial service had been asked to indicate whether they could remember some similar experience, a forest of hands would have been raised.

That was Bash – 'a prince and a great man'. No one ever more richly deserved the accolade of his Master – 'Well done, thou good and faithful servant'. That word 'faithful', when it appears in the Hebrew, is related to our word 'Amen'; and Luther in one place translates 'faithful people' as 'Amenleute' – 'the Amen-folk' or 'Yes-men'. And that is what Bash was, ever since his own conversion in his late teens, one of God's unhesitating, unfailing 'Yes-men'.

Yes, 'a prince and a great man is fallen this day'. But let us allow Daniel, another of Bash's favourite Bible characters, to have the last word: Daniel whom, as many of us will remember, he used to regard with affection and respect, and about whom he wrote a small booklet – '*The boy who dared*': Daniel who most obligingly 'purposed,' 'prayed' and 'prospered', thus furnishing Bash with the outline of one of his most famous talks: Daniel who also said this – 'They that be wise shall shine as the brightness of the firmament, and they that turn many to righteousness as the stars for ever and ever.'

2: The pioneer

Richard Rhodes-James

After serving with the Chindits in World War II, Richard Rhodes-James joined the Staff of Haileybury College, and was for many years a Housemaster there. He has recently retired from this post, and is living and working in Cambridge. In 1981 he published a book called *Chindit*, recounting his experiences in the Burma Jungle during the war.

2: The pioneer

When in 1917 Eric Nash, aged nineteen, gave his life to Christ, something very important happened. From that decision came a work that was destined to have a profound effect on the spiritual life of this nation and to make his name one that could not easily be avoided when Christian work was being discussed. It became a name spoken often with love, sometimes with awe, and occasionally with censure and even with animosity. The pioneer makes his own tracks and not everyone is willing to applaud the direction in which he is going. With no visible landmarks he must have the courage of his convictions.

His conviction was that he must evangelise the leading public schools of this country. Others had done Christian work among schoolboys. Grenfell of Labrador had run camps in Anglesey and in the Purbeck Hills, the Crusader movement was at work among the day schools, and the Scripture Union West Runton camps in Norfolk had got under way; but before long it was clear that Bash was beginning to put an entirely new stamp on boys' work.

He graduated at Trinity College, Cambridge and did his theological training at Ridley Hall. From there, after serving two curacies, he was appointed chaplain at Wrekin School. His zeal to evangelise, which he could neither conceal nor restrain, clashed with his duty to instruct, and caused uneasiness. *Conversion* was a dangerous word, as indeed it still is. There was an agreement that he should apply his gifts elsewhere. In 1932 he was appointed by the Scripture Union to work among public schoolboys. His brief experience in a public school had shown him the field in which his work was to lie. It had also shown him the peculiar difficulties of this branch of Christian work.

He had already held several holiday camps for public schoolboys. In April 1930 he led the first one, with eight other officers and thirty-three boys at Ashampstead, Seaford in Sussex. Most of the boys came from London day schools, but four were from Wrekin. In the summer of that year the camp was at St Andrew's, Eastbourne.

There were twelve officers and forty-six boys. With him as officers came two who were to give immense service in the years ahead and who both died shortly before him: Wilfred Burton, who ran the catering until the war, and Graham Leask who devoted many years of service to these camps and to the many boys who were to pass through them. They were the first indication of Bash's gift of calling forth a special brand of loyalty.

Wilfred Burton has recorded something of the flavour of those far-off days. Of the Ashampstead camp he wrote, 'Bash and I joined forces in the early summer of 1930. We had met together for prayer with two other officers. We felt that the Lord was guiding us to go forward as a team with Bash as commandant.' Of St Andrew's, Eastbourne, 'Not an easy camp. We slept in bell tents in the school grounds. Bash, in true fashion, soon obtained a bed locally! We were allowed the use of washing facilities, the dining hall and kitchen. We had an enjoyable camp, but were under the eagle eye of the resident headmaster.' In April 1931 it was Herne Bay College in Kent, with eighteen officers and seventy-eight boys. 'Famous for its drains! Sore throats resulted. So Bash and I went round each morning with bottles of Jeyes Fluid, sniffing at drains and applying disinfectant. How we laughed! Spiritually, these early camps were truly pioneering. We were being welded into a team.' The grave and the gay. Great issues and the ability to laugh at the quainter corners of God's creation.

At Herne Bay and in the summer camp of the same year at Ovingdean Hall (seventeen officers, sixty-seven boys) there was a widening in the range of schools – Winchester, Cheltenham, Shrewsbury appear. Later that year at a prayer meeting at King's College, London, Bash prayed, 'Lord, we claim the leading public schools for your kingdom.'

The next year saw the beginnings of the answers to his prayers at Temple Grove, Eastbourne (twenty-four officers, eighty-one boys) and Whitecliffe Bay, Isle of Wight (twenty-one officers, eighty-nine boys). In 1933 both Easter and Summer camps were held at King's Mead, Seaford with eighty-seven officers and one hundred and eight boys. Then in 1934 a regular pattern was established, which continued until the war, with the Easter camp at St Cyprian's, Eastbourne and the summer camp at Beachborough Park, a few miles inland from Folkestone. (By a sombre coincidence both camps suffered fire damage not long after we had moved elsewhere, St Cyprian's being gutted) The numbers mounted steadily: 1934, one hundred and fifty; 1935, one hundred and fifty nine; 1936, one hundred and sixty; 1937, one hundred and eighty-four; 1938, one hundred and ninety-four; 1939, one hundred and ninety-four. A perusal of the lists for the 1939 camps show that twenty two of the leading public schools in the country were represented.

Those pre-war days, which the writer can remember as a boy, saw the work growing steadily, propelled by an infectious enthusiasm for Christ, and a simple delight in the message that came from both the lips and life of those who gave up their time to run the camps. There was laughter and wonder and a sense that God had so much to give us and so much for us to do for him.

In 1940 it was clear that Eastbourne was no place for a camp. It lay in the path of the German bombers and possible German invaders. So Bash with others toured the south to seek a new site. They found it in the little Dorset village of Iwerne Minster, in the lovely rolling country between Blandford and Shaftesbury. The buildings that the camps were to occupy from that day on were those of Clayesmore, originally the home of a wealthy shipowner. Here we came (the writer recollects vividly that first arrival when he had just been made an officer) and here we stayed, planting the name *Iwerne* firmly in the Christian's vocabulary.

We must examine Bash's vision a little more closely. He aimed to concentrate his mission on a highly select clientele, the privileged and largely speaking the rich, who made up perhaps five per cent of our school population; not just the public schools but the top thirty or so. This was his field. He knew no other. He staked everything on this one work.

Why this intense concentration? The first answer is a simple one. These schools contained a high proportion of the future leaders of the country. Therefore to reach them with the gospel opened the possibility of reaching our future rulers, men with an immense influence over their contemporaries. A phrase often used was that our converts could be 'multiplication tables'.

Such reasoning is open to, and has been exposed to, much criticism from two quarters, from Christians and from egalitarians. The Christian response has often been: the gospel knows no class distinctions, every man is as valuable to God as any other. Indeed, to quote scripture, 'God is no regarder of persons'. To which Bash would reply with that quiet assurance that could at once mollify and frustrate, 'Yes. Of course.'

He left it to others to articulate a detailed defence of the work to which his spiritual instincts and his passion for souls was calling him. If he did not reach the leaders, who would? The fact is that the public schools were a largely unevangelised field. Others were catered for by the Boys Brigade, the Crusaders, the Pathfinders and similar organisations. No one was reaching the people who would most influence the way this country was going. Why should the top people be passed by?

In 1982 there was a lively correspondence in the *Times* about the role of public school chaplains. Should they, as one writer suggested, be ashamed of working in such a segregated field? One school chaplain wrote as follows, 'The Church should not abandon the opportunities it is given to minister to them. Many of their pupils will have positions of responsibility in adult life. Unless we believe there is no gospel for the materially better-off then to abandon our ministry would be a spiritual betrayal.' And if it is so hard for the rich to enter the Kingdom of heaven, do they not need more rather than less spiritual care and attention? Bash argued along these lines. Indeed he went further. Within the select clientele of the top thirty public schools he identified those he thought had special leadership qualities; for he was unashamed to identify quality where he thought it lay.

The egalitarians, and this included both Christians and non-Christians, attacked from another angle. Public schools were undesirable; they were divisive and bred arrogance. If you had to run camps for public schoolboys, why not mix them with boys of humbler origin so that they could see 'how the other half lived'? Bash stood absolutely firm on this. His camps were not a social exercise. They were a spiritual battleground in which a particularly difficult battle was in progress. The boys must be placed in an atmosphere in which they could feel at ease with people they understood, with a range of activities that caught their interest and imagination. It was a highly specialised operation whose success could be jeopardised by attempting to do too many things at once. Bash believed in concentrating on the spiritual objectives with a single-mindedness that not everyone could always understand.

There was another compelling reason for this work, and that lay in the nature of boarding education. The boarding school boy falls between two religious stools. He sees little of his home parish and so misses the kind of pastoral care that is available to the boy at a day school. He receives Christian teaching at school – indeed the English public schools were founded on a strong religious basis – but in an environment in which conformity is the norm and religious enthusiasm not always welcome. School religion is institutional, and although heroic efforts are made to inject meaning into both chapel and RE, circumstances are against the emergence of a strong, informed and committed Christian faith. There was a need for a work to fill the gap. And so Bash committed his life to this work.

Having seen the vision, he also saw with devastating clarity the means by which it could be realised. It involved the use of manpower more lavish than had ever before been seen in Christian work, and an attention to detail that startled those who entered the work. It also involved a total devotion to the cause.

From the start there was a very high ratio of officers to campers. With other Christian work sometimes seriously short of manpower, this has not always been easy to understand. It was due to Bash's insistence on the highest quality of pastoral work. He learnt early the lesson that the Christian world as a whole took some time to digest, that the difficult part of Christian work is not leading people to Christ but nurturing them in a faith that lasts. Counting the saved is in one sense a less significant exercise than counting the sanctified. If Bash's aim was to win Britain's leaders for Christ and his strategy was to work in the top public schools, the tactics were to lavish huge resources in the battle. This manpower Bash used to see that no boy was ever overlooked, no camp activity ever undermanned. He sought perfection and he saw its price.

It was not only quantity he sought. His officers he chose with great care. They had to meet his standards on at least three levels: totally committed Christians, totally devoted to the work of camp, able to mix and deal easily with boys between thirteen and eighteen. At camp they should be willing to take part in any activity, oversee any department, look after those in their dormitory with ceaseless care, seeing that they were happy and trying with tact and encouragement to nurture their faith. After camp they were to keep in touch by letter, recalling for the boys their fun and Christian fellowship together at a time when perhaps discouragement was wearing them down. It was a standard of 'man management' that set new patterns for Christian work.

All this gave future Christian leaders a grounding that they have acknowledged; and the present Bishops of Aston, Liverpool,

Norwich, Southwell and Thetford all passed through the Camps, and would admit their indebtedness to them and to Bash. It is an impressive list, and to it could be added well over two hundred others who are now in the ordained ministry. Bash had put his unmistakeable print on the Church of England.

He always saw his work in the light of the ultimate benefit it could bestow upon the church and the country as a whole. An admirer of his, Dr Christopher Chavasse (Bishop of Rochester from 1939-1960) was quick to appreciate its significance. He used to say that his own ministry had been spent amongst 'the many', as an army chaplain, vicar, Master of an Oxford College and Bishop; but that if he had it over again, he would feel it more important to 'work amongst the few, and give them back to the many'. There is of course excellent dominican authority for this approach, and it sums up very precisely what Bash was trying to do. Nor was it only, or even chiefly, in socially congenial spheres that his ex-campers worked; and there was a time recently when four of the best known London Clubs for young people were run by those who had been nurtured in what some may have felt to be the rather rarefied atmosphere of Iwerne Minster.

The new officer entering the officers' room for the first time saw a meticulous attention to detail. This was particularly true of the talks. The titles and the sequence of the talks were the result of endless thought and discussion. Those chosen to speak were exactly briefed and they were chosen because they came up to the required standard. Eternal truths demanded exceptional care.

Everything in camp must be right. Each day the officers met, once for prayer and once for a detailed review of how things were going, how they could be better done, how the day in question could be arranged. No issue was too small to be raised. It was God's work, and it must therefore be done properly. And on all these little things the minds of a number of able young men were concentrated. Was this extravagance? Bash did not think so. And to make sure that the paperwork was equally faultless he engaged the loyalty over a number of years of a secretary of spotless efficiency, Philip Thompson.

The most important and perhaps the most delicate part of the work was the relationship with the schools. It is from there that the camps draw their boys, it is there that the boys return and where they seek to practise their newly won faith. In the jargon of the work, it covers both recruiting and follow-up.

The delicacy of the relationship is obvious, but it took some time to learn. For an outside organisation to enter a boarding school, seek to gather boys for holiday camps and then, when they return, to visit them and sustain them spiritually requires much mutual understanding. In the early days the zeal of Bash and his helpers sometimes outran their discretion and misunderstandings arose, some of them quite serious, though in most cases they were resolved by friendly confrontations. You could not talk for long with Bash without being disarmed. Housemasters naturally wanted to know the credentials of the organisation, so that they could inform and reassure parents; and they would not be happy to find that their charges had been taken out by strangers without leave. School chaplains did not want to feel that their own work was being by implication criticised. Bash quickly learnt that in this Christian work, while the gospel is free, the way in which it is spread abroad can have at times quite severe constraints.

Bash also learnt that, if he was to win the confidence of the schools among which he worked, the surest way was to have as his officers those who taught at these schools. It was a plan that has had a quite remarkable success. Somewhere around one hundred and fifty of those who have helped to run the camps have taught or are still teaching at public schools. A number of these have become housemasters, and six have become headmasters. This has given the camps a secure base from which to operate, and it has reassured the schools themselves about an organisation that has puzzled many and antagonised a few. At times when there were dark words about emotional pressures, it was reassuring to know that the camps were staffed at least in part by remarkably sane men, most with a well developed sense of humour. It has also given to the schools a body of men who are not only committed to a strong Christian faith at a time of increasing spiritual uncertainty, but who have also infused the schools with a sense of vocation and pastoral concern that has been more and more recognised and appreciated.

Bash's vision, and the logic of his work, took him in other directions. When these boys left school, what would happen to them? It was assumed, rightly in many cases, that they would go to university, probably Oxford or Cambridge. Their faith must be nurtured, too. From 1944 Bash started inviting undergraduates to camp to continue the teaching they had received at past camps, or in some cases inviting them there for the first time through contacts made at Oxford and Cambridge. In 1950 there came an important development, the creation of the 'senior camper'. They were largely undergraduates. They came to help, to do the chores that a camp demands, to serve tables, but also to receive teaching geared to their age and experience. An increasing number of people found their faith at university, and many of them came to Iwerne. In 1957 there were no fewer than one hundred and forty-five, in 1977 one hundred and thirty-nine and since then about eighty a year.

Many of them became officers, some of them went to other Christian work, all received teaching at a time when they most needed it. Back at the university they continued to receive spiritual guidance from camp officers and encouragement from each other. On arriving at the university they often found that the first to greet them were those whom they had known at Iwerne. Bash's vision of a complete Christian work was becoming a reality.

In the war years, when many enterprises had to cease, the camps at Iwerne thrived as they had never done before. This was due largely to the fact that they undertook farming and forestry which the country at war demanded and which parents were only too willing for their sons to participate in. Numbers grew. In the Easter and summer camps of 1941 there were two hundred and twenty-six, in 1942 two hundred and sixty-one, in 1943 three hundred and thirty-one. Numbers remained around the two hundred mark, rising in 1948 to three hundred and twenty-two.

The work widened further. Winter camps were started, largely to consolidate the evangelistic work of the summer and Easter camps and to build up young Christians. From 1941 these took place at Iwerne, but Iwerne is hardly cosy in January, and in 1960 it shifted to Eastbourne. In 1962 it split into two separate houseparties, one for sixth formers and one for undergraduates. There were few 'activities'. The young men went there to be instructed in the faith. To the charge that the camps exposed adolescents to emotional pressures, Bash could reply that he was submitting them to more solid teaching than any other comparable Christian work.

Growing numbers caused the Easter camp to be split into two in 1949, when the total at Easter was one hundred and five, and in 1955 the summer camps were increased from two to three, though sadly that year the third camp had to be cancelled because of an outbreak of glandular fever. The numbers at Easter have dropped quite sharply in recent years for a number of reasons. Summer numbers reached a peak in 1976 and 1977 of two hundred and eighty-three and two hundred and eighty-five, declining since to about one hundred and eighty-five.

In 1945 the logic of the work took an important turn. Where did the public schoolboys come from? Until quite recently the answer was straightforward – from the preparatory schools. So a complete Christian work for the top strata of our society must start here. In 1945 John Eddison (who first came as a camper to the Isle of Wight in 1932) started his preparatory school camps at Bude with thirty-two boys. By 1950 there were two separate camps and the work settled at Swanage. Numbers reached their peak in 1975 when there were three hundred and fourteen boys and four consecutive camps. Since then numbers have fallen a little and there are again just three camps. The inspiration for this work came from Bash's original vision. Many of those who help in these camps are themselves preparatory schoolmasters. John Eddison relinquished command of this work in 1981 and handed over to Tim Sterry, who gave up the headmastership of a preparatory school and took over the leadership.

Iwerne gave birth to other children. If Iwerne itself was to cover the top public schools, what about the others? There were plenty, and they needed Christ. In 1947 Bash was asked to take over the West of England Scripture Union camp. This he did and gave the leadership to Chandos Morgan, later to become Chaplain of the Fleet. He took six officers and twenty boys to Bude. The camp moved to a variety of locations until it came to rest for a number of years at Stoodleigh Court near Tiverton in Devon in 1952 under Anthony Creery-Hill. Finally it settled in Lymington, first under Richard Hovil until 1971, then Clive Sampson and now David Harris. From the mid-fifties a junior camp has been run and 'senior campers' came in during the sixties. The familiar and tried patterns of Iwerne became the norm.

These camps catered largely for the London day schools, and others that could be said to be outside the 'top thirty'. It was a sub-division that showed how precise Bash's strategies were. Not only did it enable like to meet like at camp, but it also made easier the work of keeping in touch with the campers afterwards. For those outside the work this might seem a refinement of the élitism of

Iwerne, a first and a second division. It was in fact another example of a specialisation that sought to achieve the best for all.

The Lymington camps developed in other directions. There was a measure of fragmentation: walking parties in the Lakes, Wales, Scotland, Yugoslavia, and in 1971 a mixed camp for sixth formers. In one sense these activities went against Bash's own ideas. He was unwilling to have too many 'spin-offs' in case these pulled away too many from the main camps where Christian teaching could take place free of distractions. He also never contemplated having girls. But within the looser framework which developed Bash's basic ideas continued: total commitment, ceaseless care, close attention to detail. These camps were also able to use some of the huge flow of Christian workers that poured out of Iwerne.

Another work emerged in 1966, designed to deal with a geographical problem. Iwerne drew its campers very much from the south of England, and the north and midlands were largely untouched. This territory must be claimed. In that year Peter Marshall, who was to mastermind the operation, took thirty-two preparatory schoolboys with eight officers to St David's College, Gloddaeth, Llandudno. It grew fast. By 1967 there were two junior camps of about forty boys each at Llandudno. In order to hold their junior campers, now at public schools, they held an Easter activity in 1970, a community service project in Liverpool. Just ten boys attended, but the work has continued in different needy places until today.

It was time to start on the older boys. In 1971 came the first senior camp at Llandudno. By 1973 there were thirty-six seniors and one hundred juniors. The work then spread east to Bridlington with a party of thirty-one boys. In 1976 there was a sixteen plus mixed party led by Michael and Jane Tupper, a small pilot scheme which promised well. By 1980 both age groups were mixed and the work developed further. There are now six summer camps, three senior and three junior, of which two are in Bridlington and four in North Wales. In 1982 they were attended by some two hundred and fifty boys and girls from schools stretching from the Isle of Man to York. Peter Marshall writes, 'Needless to say that the influence of Bash is stamped firmly on our camps, the ABC of the gospel, the preaching of the cross, the importance of sound doctrine and faithful long term follow-up'.

Bash's intention was that his camp should be limited to boys. At no time did he envisage the presence of girls, and at the time of writing Iwerne remains committed to this stance. But there were others who saw what these camps were doing among the top boys' public schools and saw the possibilities among the girls' schools. In the summer of 1953 three wives, newly married to Iwerne officers, paid their first visit to Iwerne. One of them, Mary Mullins, was to attend forty consecutive camps and to take over the girls' work. In the autumn of 1955 the women got together to plan. If the public schoolboys were the future leaders, what about their wives? And how could Christian families be raised? Where could 'top girls' hear the gospel? It might be too late when they left school and got swept into the whirl of London social life.

The first girls' camp, a very wet one, was held in the Lake District in August 1956 with Margaret Butterworth as leader helped by Margaret Saunders (née Talbot-Rice) and Mary Mullins and with eighteen girls. In 1957 the camp moved to Chagford in Devon and in 1960 with a move to Lavant House, Chichester, Mary Mullins took over the leadership. In 1971 the camp moved to Motcombe Park in North Dorset, where it was destined to stay for a number of years. There were fifty girls, fifteen senior members (the girls' equivalent of senior campers) and twenty-five officers. In 1972 the first junior camp was set up with twenty-five girls. In 1982 there were over fifty girls at the senior camps, twenty senior members and thirty-three officers. There is now a travelling secretary who visits the girls during the term. The pattern set at Iwerne has been followed closely.

This was the remarkable family that Bash fathered. Over seven thousand boys have passed through Iwerne alone and many hundreds in other camps. Bash retired officially in 1965 and handed over to David Fletcher, who has continued to carry out and develop the methods that he pioneered. Bash himself continued to come to Iwerne, to speak and to counsel and to reflect with what must have been profound gratitude how God had used him down the years. His name appeared for the last time in the address lists in summer 1979.

Others have taken up the work that Bash started those many years ago. They have made changes to suit the passing years, the changing tastes and interests of the public schoolboy, refusing to get stuck in a cultural posture or a frozen idea. But they have also refused to relinquish the principles that Bash pioneered: concentration on a carefully chosen objective, meticulous attention at every stage and in every detail of the operation, the ceaseless care of those in their charge and total faithfulness to the gospel. Some have questioned these methods; none have been able to deny their fruit.

3: The man of God

Dick Lucas

After war-time service in the Royal Navy, Dick Lucas trained at Cambridge for the Ministry, and became a curate at Sevenoaks. For several years he worked for the Church Pastoral-Aid Society, and during that time he had a lot to do with launching the camps that are now held at Lymington. He left the CPA to become Rector of St Helen's, Bishopsgate, and as well as his work in the city, he has many invitations to speak at missions and conferences in different parts of the world.

3: The man of God

My first impression of 'Bash' was of his personal sanctity. This may seem an odd word to use (a risky one too as I shall show later) and a strange reaction from a fifteen-year-old, but I must tell things as they were. I had travelled down to his boys' 'camp' in the summer holidays of 1941, more or less under compulsion, since some kind of harvesting or similar activity was expected of schoolboys as part of the war effort; and a chance invitation to a schools' party in Dorset seemed to offer the pleasantest way of doing it. In my pockets were cheap cigarettes, painful signs of teenage non-conformity which – I blush as I write – were offered to the smiling leaders who welcomed me.

Bash, as the commandant (for some reason military titles were used widely in such youth work) was rather in the background, so it was these helpers of his who first impressed me by their friendliness, concern, and, as I came to know them, by their remarkable abilities and gifts.

Despite the daily slog up the hill to clear woodland – I made a nuisance of myself by bringing down a tree, fortunately only a sapling, on the head of the estate's owner – I can recall only the fun of the whole thing, and that, curiously enough, included daily 'prayers'. These, obviously and unapologetically, were the centre of 'camp' life. Many of the truths I must have known before, but now the whole Christian scheme began to fit together, beautifully and coherently, and before time was out my heart had been opened willingly to the Christ of whom, each day, we heard. Failure back at school followed with humiliating speed, but true foundations had been well laid, so that, later on during naval service, I returned to spiritual reality. Since then a lifetime of Christian service has proved that, by God's mercy, a work was begun in me during that August harvest camp forty years ago. As I look back momentarily to record this, it seems a great deal clearer to me how much I owe to the singular man behind it all.

As I have said, it was Bash's sanctity that first made its mark. It is a mistake to think that boisterous teenagers with grubby habits can see no attraction in goodness. For myself, anglo-catholic influence at school had led me to some admiration for spiritual devotedness of life, yet it had never seemed 'earthed', so that religion as taught appeared to be untransferrable to real life. It was at school, too, with its many chapel services, that I began a life-time's suspicion of 'churchiness', as too often exhibited by boys who formed the chaplain's inner core of assistants. Not that I disliked chapel services myself – I was never a rebel in that way – for a good sing, an escape into an atmosphere of peace and beauty, an occasional emotional 'lift', the sense of a great heritage, all these were comparatively sweet fruits in the not very Christian society of a big school. But looking back I can see that it was a form of religion, with sadly little power to assure of divine forgiveness or alter one's selfish ways.

'Camp' changed all that. The Gospel of Christ, simply explained, demonstrated its power. And in the leaders, particularly in Bash himself, I saw that close walk with God which is so wonderfully compelling. 'Sanctity' is of course a dangerous word to describe something which, in the best sense, is so unpretentious and normal, simply because foolish people will confuse it with quite another thing, 'sanctimoniousness', something from which Bash was, quite exceptionally, free. No man ever hankered less for 'long robes, greetings in the market place, and the best seats in the synagogue.' 'Church' was not his special interest. It might even be said that he had something of that gaucherie C. S. Lewis confessed to finding in himself that makes a person unapt to participate in rites and ceremonies. This is not to say that he was ungifted in the leadership of prayer and praise. Not for him (horrors!) sitting on a table swinging legs and cracking jokes, before 'a word of prayer' in order to win acceptability and impress the young with one's 'sincerity.' It is simply impossible to imagine his becoming 'one of the boys', a maddening habit I was to meet later amongst certain service chaplains and others working amongst men. With Bash, The Daily Prayers were carried out with quite dignity and simplicity, combined with a reality that could be awesome, and was certainly impressive to me who had met nothing like it in years of church going.

But it would be a mistake to concentrate too exclusively on Bash's unquestioned spirituality, in a narrow sense, as an explanation of his influence. There was in him a remarkable combination of qualities, attitudes, and abilities which, sometimes misunderstood by friends as well as foes, could seem 'unspiritual', yet were, in my view, essential to his success. I often recall a conversation with the senior chaplain of a boarding school where I had preached one Sunday evening. He had been a contemporary of Bash's at Cambridge and conversation came round to those days. It was immediately apparent that Bash's fame was something of an irritating enigma to him. Perhaps his puzzlement was due to the fact that, only coming in touch with boys late in life, he was largely ineffective among them, which made it harder to recognize how one so seemingly unimpressive as Eric Nash the undergraduate could have won such influence among young people. Since then I have often pondered on that conversation and realised how commonly Bash was given little credit for what were quite rare qualities of personality. This is not to deny that God delights to use us in our weakness, but it is to deny that the God who called this particular young man to do an outstanding work took pains to prepare and equip his chosen instrument. It must be of value to try to discover some of these God-given talents so that, so far as in us lies, we may follow his example. Let me mention some at least.

First there was his *realism,* an almost ruthless ability to see things as they really are, rather than as sentiment, convention, prejudice or regard for good form, might dictate how they should be seen. For example he recognised that most clergymen were ill-equipped in practical spiritual ministries – are still – and that evangelicals in particular were often hindered by lack of education. (This clarity of insight is reminiscent of 'Monty' whose cold assessments of the troops' need of training whenever and wherever he took command is well known: incidentally Bash had other Monty-like qualities such as the extraordinary confidence that defeat was out of the question if you fought according to his plan, so that coming into his presence your morale lifted immediately, and you could not imagine why hitherto you had been so dreary and doubting). The training he gave to his team of helpers in practical terms was far ahead of anything the training colleges were offering. He could be merciless in a constructive way, and no concessions to good manners would hinder a frank appraisal of your person, performance, clothes or habits.

Then, too, he recognised, quite without illusions, but also without cynicism, the parlous state of the Church in England. ('The shepherds of my people have lost their senses; they no longer follow God nor ask his will. Therefore . . . their flocks are scattered' Jer. 10:21). His answer to the feebleness and falsity apparent everywhere was not to opt out in despair (among young idealists, 'dropping out' in disgust had not yet become a popular attitude as it was later to become in many areas of life), but to encourage a host of boys and young men to enter the ranks of the ordained ministry.

Realism also pointed to the fact that 'public school religion' as generally practised had few serious claims to be a power in young people's lives, and indeed was often hostile to any living expression of faith. This was especially so in his early days before there was a more sympathetic understanding of his purposes, as well as a growing number of spiritually-minded headmasters; and it explains why his early visits to schools were more in the nature of invading enemy territory.

Now realism like this can never be popular, is disconcerting to live with, and is certainly not easy to maintain with regard to one's own treasured concerns. But I think it will be found to explain much of his success and many of his decisions in the greatest days. To take a case at random, he clung on to a 'camp' site and daily programme that seemed dull compared with the ever more exciting holidays on offer to an increasingly affluent society because he wanted a full spiritual programme with boys sufficiently awake in the evenings to attend to it. Many of us must have organised church holidays in which the all consuming demands of ski-ing, or fell-walking or whatever, have meant that people have little strength left over to give to what was originally meant to be the whole point of the exercise. At one such ski-ing party where I was chaplain I recall having to stay up until 2 a.m. and later to get any chance of a good conversation with the vigorous young men who skied all day and après-skied all night. At Bash's parties, as every schoolboy knows – and I imagine this never changed – it was early to bed and late to rise so that everyone, including the commandant, got his nine hours refreshing sleep.

Linked with this realism I would mention his *shrewdness*. Bash was no scholar, nor much interested in the cultural side of life; perhaps, with so many other things, this latter had been purposefully put aside long ago in order to concentrate on the one thing needful. But really I think Florence, Greece or even the Mediterranean sun, meant little to him; Eastbourne and Worthing were sufficient. But whatever can be said along these lines (and a latent anti-intellectualism, although fully understandable in the between-war years of raging liberalism may have been an impoverishment) it was always the greatest mistake to dismiss his opinions or fail to give them a careful hearing. He had an uncanny knack of seeing to the heart of things, and he well illustrated the lesson that it is safer to follow the instincts of men like him than the intellects of much cleverer men. This was so of his assessments of current and fashionable opinions to which all others were deferring, of his judgment of people and their motives, his ability to read situations, and above all of his genius for seeing precisely what was necessary to reach through the defences of the hardest and most stubborn person. I think of one very clever boy, later killed in a mountain accident, who easily withstood the claims of what he was hearing until, at a last opportunity, Bash walked and talked with him one night after prayers. How well I recall that evening! Few men knew more surely the way into a boy's heart, yet even he needed all his exceptional gifts to lead that brilliant boy out of the dark mazes of self-deception, pride and agnosticism, into the clear light of faith.

This shrewdness also showed itself in his choice of leaders. No doubt those who were regarded as in some way unsuitable could sometimes find him unfeeling, since here, as in much besides, he was entirely without sentimentalism. In this he made an interesting contrast with another godly evangelical leader of a previous generation, Bishop Handley Moule. According to a famous passage in Hensley Henson's Reminiscences, Moule was notoriously weak in resisting unsuitable candidates for ordination, being particularly malleable in the case of the blind and other physically disadvantaged. 'I remember how on one occasion when, during my tenure of the Deanship, Bishop Moule came to the Cathedral for an Ordination, and the candidates were more than usually and apparently unpromising, I caused a brief disturbance of his accustomed urbanity by observing, "Bishop, when you come here for an Ordination, the Cathedral acquires the aspect of the Pool of Bethesda."' My guess is that while Bash would have been less impressed with Henson than with the saintly, if unbusiness-like Moule, he would certainly have been unwilling to allow sentiment to dictate who was suitable for the special responsibilities of the work he was engaged in. That he turned away good men is probable, but it is likely that he was usually right that their gifts lay elsewhere than in 'camp' work.

Then there was his *courage*. For instance, he found himself with a gift for the single life, and found also in Scripture that this was an equally valid option to marriage for the Christian worker, good in

God's eyes, and specially useful in certain areas of service. But in the climate of his day it needed courage to say so, and he was freely criticized for his stand, and its influence upon others. There was in him a seemingly inhuman independence of the opinions of others, and for all I know he cared not a fig what was said about him. Nevertheless, whether or not it was easy for him to stand alone, it is unquestionably true that this exceptional independence of outlook was a strength.

An amusing illustration of this unselfconscious refusal to worry about what others might think of him comes to mind. I was with him in a 'camp' leaders' meeting at Scripture Union HQ when the discussion was on a revision of a widely used hymn book. Quite properly there was a strong move to oust from the new revision some weak tunes and verses. But Bash who had no musical taste or poetic skills was determined to keep a number of greatly used old favourites; perhaps, too, that sharp sense of smell sniffed out the scent of musical snobbery in some who professed themselves committed to drastic change. Needless to say he fought a good fight. But most astonishing to the assembled company was the moment when he burst out into a tuneless rendering of 'Dear Saviour, thou art mine'. What people's reactions might be never seemed to enter his head; and needless to say, such tactics were somewhat confusing to the other side.

This courage to be himself I judge to have been one of the biggest strengths. It has been said that his work tended to turn out stereotyped Christians ('It's not a bad type', he used to protest); but whatever truth lies in this criticism – and a similar boarding school background may have something to do with it – one is bound to insist that it would be really impossible to copy Bash himself. True there were certain traits in him such as his bright way of talking to children that he had seen and admired in Hudson Pope, a famous children's worker, and which others in turn have picked up from him. But his own distinctive flavour remained inimitable. Bash was surely *sui generis,* genuinely unclassifiable. How unlikely that any writer of fiction could have set down so improbable a creature! How vain the attempt, without absurdity, to copy him!

This distinctiveness was valuable in another way. He simply did not 'fit in' with the generality. In his early days, workers among youth were expected to be rather noisy and jocular, turning somersaults in and out of swimming baths, swathed in athletic garments or dotted with badges of sporting supremacy. In the twenties and thirties 'bloodery' was not yet on the ebb tide. Heartiness reigned. But how much Bash disliked all that! He never despised in boys their need to play and let off steam; games and laughter were to be had in abundance. Actually he liked 'gamesy' boys, as he called them, because he had got it into his head that they made good Christian workers. But though his own impish sense of humour was a constant delight to his leaders, guffawing and horse-play in camp life were severely discouraged. He himself played few games in my time, but when he did participate in 'padder' (a kind of miniature tennis) it was with a characteristic kind of restrained refinement.

Realism, shrewdness, fearlessness – these were three outstanding qualities, and as I write many others start emerging from memory's files and demanding to be mentioned such as his single-minded pursuit of chosen goals. But other contributors will fill out the picture. Let me finish by saying something I've long felt, that Bash was essentially a 'strong' man, even if in the eyes of the world he seemed weak and of no account. The Pastoral Epistles make much of this quality of *strength* as indispensable in the Pastor. 'Able to control his own household', 'Able to confute those in error and stop damaging talk', are indicative of the necessary personal authority. Bash was certainly master in his own work, though surrounded by many able men. Few of us were not in some awe of his letters with their requests and rebukes. Should a boy he had once influenced become an Archbishop, even he could not expect to be spared a demand or a polite drubbing: 'Dear Bill (or whoever), the letter would inimitably run, 'you've become a big man now, and I wish you would set an example by. . .' and then would follow criticisms and suggestions without fear or favour.

Paul also insists of Timothy and Titus that the leaders they select must have no big weaknesses, or flaws in their character, either in the realms of drink, money, sex or temper. Bash hated alcohol, coveted only a Rover to take him purring round the countryside on school visits, and was a man of the strictest purity and self-control.

Truly, God made him a giant in spiritual stature, a strong man in leadership, and a man of steel in the face of evil. This great and unfaltering strength was matched, no doubt through the divine sense of proportion (on earth we might call this the other side of a sense of humour), by one or two quaint weaknesses. Were these at first exaggerated by himself almost as a means of not taking himself too seriously? He was the supreme pricker of bubbles and general deflater of pretentiousness, and it would fit one's idea of him if he first practised this art on himself. But by degrees he was stuck with them, as for example, the hypochondriacal spirit that took him on a ceaseless quest to chemists and doctor friends, seeking the elixir of life. I suppose this was partly a Victorian hangover; he ought to have married someone like Gwen Raverat's Aunt Etty who gloried in other people's illnesses and regularly covered her husband, Uncle Richard, in a sheet whenever the windows were briefly opened, in order to protect him from draughts (Period Piece: Faber & Faber). Once, in his old age, I yielded to his importunity and took him by car to Eastbourne on a summer's day. Foolishly I told him that, due to exhaust trouble, he might smell fumes if we braked hard on a steep hill. This led to his spending the entire journey with windows wide open and a finger under his nose while, increasingly irritated, I urged him to remember that sudden death meant sudden glory.

There will be special moments in the future when I shall greatly miss him; such will be when speaking to some student audience; a familiar figure would slip into the back of the big building, half-an-hour late, and sit there as though not belonging to the meeting, the long neck emerging out of the thick flannel shirt collar like a tortoise from its shell, the thin face peering impassively here and there, the hooded eyes blinking complacently at the sight of some 'wounded bird' who should be followed up, or a 'camper' surrounded with non-Christian friends obviously doing his stuff. But I must confess it will be a bit of relief not to get a letter two mornings later pointing out that while he went home all the way to Maidenhead saying 'Hooray', he thought the talk missed out on the key point of the gospel and might have been shorter.

As I write about him I begin to realise afresh how much the church owes to him and as well the greatness of my own debt. I wish I had written to tell him so: I think he would have been pleased, but also quaintly embarrassed. He never knew how to react to praise.

Hensley Henson, OUP '*Retrospect of an Unimportant Life 1863-1939*' Vol. One. p. sixty-nine.

4: The prayer warrior

David Fletcher

David Fletcher first came to Iwerne Minster while an undergraduate at Oxford, and after serving a curacy with Maurice Wood at Islington, he joined the Staff of Scripture Union to work in the independent schools with Bash. In 1967 he took over the leadership of Iwerne Minster from Bash, and when John Eddison retired at the end of 1980, David became responsible for all the Scripture Union work in the independent schools.

4: The prayer warrior

Bash once quoted to me 'The source of every work of God can be traced to one kneeling figure'. He said it quite unselfconsciously. It was clear to me that as far as the work of Iwerne was concerned, he was that kneeling figure. And yet he knew that the work of an intercessor was given in an especial way to certain people, of whom he felt he was one. Bash himself was a child of prayer: both his parents were praying people, but it was his aunt who told him she had prayed for him every day since he was born.

A man's prayer life is most secret and one can only glean what Bash's was like from little comments he made about himself and his own practice in public and teaching on prayer.

Like Jesus and John, he taught people to pray. Many prayed aloud for the first time in Bash's presence, after encouragement from him and an example of simple intimate prayer. Others have caught the vision of intercessory prayer as, in company with Bash, people, opportunities, challenges and problems have one by one been prayed through with him.

After his own conversion, on the 6.5 train from London to Maidenhead on February 17th, 1917, quite quietly and unostentatiously, his delight would be to go for a walk in the evening and pray as he walked.

Later, he told me, he did much of his praying in the evening late, but he found this prevented sleep and so in the fifties, at least when I knew him, it was between the hours of seven and nine in the morning that was his principal time of prayer. Not, of course, that that was the only time he prayed. Sometimes he would be burdened for an hour to pray for someone – and he would have expected that person might have been similarly burdened for him. At other times he would be sitting quietly in his room with his small looseleaf notebook open at the list of officers coming to the next camp, praying for each one. At other times he would say, 'I am going to have a bit of a blotto' and you knew that he wanted to get away to pray. He never prayed all night. He felt he would not be able to – and was so glad to discover that one of his great heroes R.A. Torrey admitted to falling asleep when trying to do so. Besides all this, there was the continual commitment of people and opportunities as they arose. One officer, a county cricket player, was due to play during camp. He was slightly injured and couldn't play – to the supposed gratification of Bash. 'You've been praying, Mr. Nash' was the accusation I heard. Later I asked Bash 'Did you pray about it?' 'No' he said, 'I just committed it (in prayer) when I first heard about it.' On another occasion as he was sitting in his car outside a school, the boys were walking past. 'Lord, save these boys' Bash suddenly prayed. There has since been a remarkable revival in that school.

People have imagined he prayed only for his own work; but this is not true. Once he told us about his weekly prayer list. We guessed he only told us a tenth of it, but on Sundays, he said, to our surprise and amusement, he prayed for Kruschev, the Russian leaders and peace in the world. Not so long ago, after visiting us at home, as our daughter said goodbye, he said to us 'Would you mind if I put her on my prayer list and prayed for her?'

Because Bash's life was so steeped in prayer, many had a glimpse of that prayer life as he prayed with them, either alone or in prayer meetings. One Christian said to me 'I talk with (he mentioned a Christian worker) and feel encouraged. I have a time of prayer with Bash and I feel all my problems solved in the presence of Jesus'. Bash would share others' prayer burdens with them: praying with them for their particular needs. He would delight at times to pray with somebody through some of the great chapters of the Bible on the cross, like Psalm 22 or Isaiah 53. In his praying two notes were struck. One of devotion to Jesus 'We come to thee as lovers of thine'. The other was that of business. 'We come to do business with thee Lord Jesus'. Sometimes 'business' – prayer business – was done first 'to get it out of the way so to speak', before other simple delights of living were sampled.

Although he prayed much, he eschewed lengthy prayers. Whereas Moody would interrupt a brother's prayer with the announcement of a hymn, Bash would do it with an 'amen' while the pray-er was pausing for breath. In speaking from John 17 Bash delighted to point out that when Jesus prayed he addressed his Father simply as 'Abba' and reverently 'Abba Father'. Bash rather deprecated the longwinded titles given to the Almighty by some in their public prayers, preferring the more straightforward 'Lord', or 'Lord Jesus', or

'Master'. At the same time he deplored any irreverence that might be implied, either by word or by position of the body.

A feature of his own praying, and one which he encouraged in others was what the Puritans called 'suing God for his promise'. He would love in prayer to claim the fulfilment of Biblical promises: his prayers would be framed round such a promise and he would plead for its fulfilment, or he would quote a statement from the Bible and argue from that for a particular request to be granted.

An invariable request in prayer at Camp was that God would raise up another Wesley to stalk the land. Before visits to a school his request often was that God would give him one contact to make and follow-up.

His conviction that prayer was the key to spiritual blessing was so strong that he believed – as he put it once – that if an owl preached the gospel on an occasion where there was much prayer, there would be fruit.

Bash not only had the gift of personal evangelism to such an extent that Bible class leaders would ring him up and ask him to come over to them to lead a boy to Christ, but he also had the gift of picking up and following up new Christians.

I remember well meeting him for the first time. From my point of view I was going to be invited to Iwerne. From his point of view I was being 'vetted'. He didn't stay long, but returned quite soon to ask me out to tea the following week. Of course I persuaded him to have tea with me. I discovered from his friends that he had certain definite likes and dislikes as far as tea was concerned (non-pippy jam or honey, brown bread, marzipan cake and cucumber). I determined to get all of them in, feign ignorance of his taste and see the reaction.

'I've only got brown bread' I apologised, 'I hope that's all right'.

'O, yes, fine'.

'I'm a bit short of stuff to put on it – would honey do?'

'O, yes, I like honey'.

'I've got some marzipan cake: I hope you like it'.

'O, yes, I'm fond of marzipan cake.'

So far there was no trace of secrets having been revealed, but now something really odd had to be produced.

'I went out shopping and passed a greengrocer and found this rather good looking cucumber – would that interest you at all?'

'Who has been telling you about me?' he asked with a laugh and mock indignation.

I felt here was a man of character who could have his leg pulled. But, of course, by far the better part of the time was when he suggested that we should read together. He had not got a Bible with him so I had to borrow one from someone upstairs ('He didn't mind, I hope' said Bash) and we read 1 Thessalonians 5. He told me later that I had described it in a letter as 'a precious time'.

The ability not only quickly to win a person's confidence, but also of being able to nip into a person's room, read and pray with him, and slip out again was greatly used in building up new Christians.

One point of prayer Bash never seemed to have made was his successor, although he knew that John Eddison was ready to step into his shoes, should he be run over by a bus. The reason for this was that he never envisaged retiring. When the Scripture Union wanted him to retire from the Staff at the age of sixty-five, he pointed out to their Chairman in very clear tones that he was at the height of his powers and that Winston Churchill was winning the war at that age.

He got a reprieve until the age of sixty-seven – but he continued to lead Iwerne until he was seventy, at which age the S.U. said he must step down and I was to take over. There was talk of not allowing him to come to Iwerne for a year, to make a break, but he would never have stood for that.

Against all experience in other fields, Bash's presence at Iwerne while his successor took over was never a hindrance or difficulty but always a help. If ever he revealed his self-discipline it was in this area. He supported me most loyally; and after camp was over he would write and thank me for the privilege of serving under me. There were many times when I planned to do things which he would never have done and which went contrary to his way of doing things; but he always backed me and often suggested ways of doing them better. He continued coming to Iwerne into his eighties.

Bash did kneel in prayer – but not often: his position was sometimes sitting, but more often lying on his bed. The sources of the blessing of Iwerne can be traced to that recumbent figure.

5: The speaker

Dick Knight

After serving in the army throughout the war, Dick Knight became an assistant master at Marlborough College, and later a Housemaster. In 1956 he was appointed Headmaster of Oundle, a post he held for twelve years, before leaving to become Headmaster of Monkton Combe. He is now living in active retirement in Bath.

5: The speaker

'Never man spoke as this man speaks' – such was the verdict of the Jewish temple police on Jesus. The seventh chapter of St John's Gospel, from which the well-known quotation comes, giving a fascinating picture of our Lord at work – quietly teaching, patiently answering questions, shamelessly and authoritatively establishing his own claims, confidently guaranteeing the satisfaction of their deepest needs to all who will 'come to me'. No wonder people listened! no wonder the police found it impracticable to make an arrest! no wonder they accorded to the speaker this accolade of uniqueness!

The writer is one of many who have been privileged over the past forty-odd years to listen regularly to talks from Bash; and it is no exaggeration to say that we would feel no impropriety in using similar words of him. Had the word been 'preached' or 'lectured', or 'argued', no-one would claim unusual or outstanding achievement for him. In earlier years, admittedly, he did occasionally preach to large congregations – The writer recalls a sermon at a packed nave service in Norwich Cathedral – and he certainly often occupied pulpits in churches and school chapels; these, however, were unusual occasions, undertaken often with reluctance by a man whose voice was never strong and who tended to find large crowds uncongenial. But put him in an undergraduate's room with an audience, say, of twenty young men prepared to be interested in the basic Christian doctrines and their application to modern life; or in the library at his beloved Iwerne Minster confronted with hundred-odd teenagers; and he was unsurpassed. 'How *does* he do it?' was a question posed again and again at the close of such sessions, after a miscellaneous group of intelligent and extrovert schoolboys and undergraduates had listened spellbound to what an unthinking critic might well have dismissed as a rather self-evident if not 'corny' presentation of Christian beliefs.

How, then, *did* he do it? How is it that so many of his friends can look back down the years and recall the rapt attention with which successive generations of such audiences listened to him in the impressionable and formative years of their young manhood? Many of those hearers within a few years were leaders of English life – politicians, high-ranking service officers, men prominent in their professions or in industry; a large number were ordained, and a rapid 'count' brings to mind at least seven bishops, four heads of theological colleges and numerous headmasters. And it was not simply that these young men listened at the time and accepted the message with gratitude; for very many the impact of these addresses, reinforced by the pastoral care which followed, persisted through their lives. Moreover – and this is no mean achievement – even those who felt this particular challenge was not for them were impressed by the graciousness and sincerity of the speaker, and very rarely went away embittered. In short, Bash was a speaker who left some convinced, many thoughtful and few resentful.

It is usually hard to disentangle the threads which compose a sound cord, and in any attempt to distinguish the various strands which made these addresses so powerful one problem is that they were by their nature generally unrecorded and perhaps unrecordable. As so often it was the attractiveness of the speaker's personality, reinforcing the phrasing and the arguments, which gave his words their unusual impact. In fact, on the rare occasions when a talk was taped and replayed, the effect – for many at least – was unimpressive and occasionally ludicrous. There is of course never a substitute for the living word; and this was more true than ever in Bash's case. Recorded, or produced in pamphlet form, his addresses lose their vigour and freshness; and this makes the ingredients the harder to sort out.

However – to make an attempt – most of his hearers would probably agree, as they review their own memories, that certain characteristics can be identified. One is certainly *simplicity;* another *clarity;* a third *authority* (though with an engaging absence of arrogance). And many would rate *relevance* (a determination to gear the message to his audience's ways of thought) as the most marked and significant of all.

To take the last of these points first; it was no doubt the overmastering desire to reach his hearers with his message that inclined Bash to prefer the small arena of drawing-room or library to that of hall or church. He was happiest, too, with the homogeneous audience, so that he could speak without apology or qualification, 'to their condition'; he was at his best with a group of intelligent sixth-formers or undergraduates. Given this 'platform', all the charm of his personality would be exercised to win attention and a fair hearing – with remarkable success. Indeed, to many it was his ability to do this which surprised most of all. There was no pretence of scholarliness, or of theological profundity – though he knew parts of his Bible intimately, and could apply them with disconcerting appositeness. His concern for social problems and international affairs was not specially deep; though he studied the issues enough to talk good sense to a group of young men to whom such things mattered a great deal. He was no kind of athlete himself; though, aware of the interest many of his hearers would usually take in sporting contests, he regularly tried to take a similar interest himself (even to the length – in earlier years – of attending matches at Stamford Bridge), so that he could at least profess common enthusiasms with them. In short, his points of contact with the audience were rather superficial; and we may add that his very personal appearance was unimpressive, so that many on first introduction were inclined to underrate his appeal. But give him his head, and allow him to make his points, and again and again initial impressions were adjusted and the graciousness and persuasiveness of the speaker won attention for his message. There was, in fact, an engaging and reassuring winsomeness about Bash as he urged his familiar points, and few could hear him without the growing conviction that this was a man who could speak with relevance of the greatest issues of life. Not that he watered his message or pulled his punches; he would ruthlessly expose the pretences and shams with which most of us seek to justify ourselves. But he always spoke with love as well as with understanding; and even while we squirmed at the uncanny knack with which his finger found the sorest spots, we never doubted that his powers were used wholly for good. A contemporary critic of the Roman satirist Horace says that 'he skilfully exposes every fault to his friend – who still smiles'. And I have often reflected how we too, as we listened to his exposure of our condition, smiled as we suffered.

And the points he repeatedly urged were simplicity itself; the very basic tenets of the Christian gospel. Man's need; God's provision in Christ; the possibility of forgiveness followed by a life of discipleship. His instincts taught him that these were the essentials, so badly needed by most of his hearers, and he was reluctant to go far beyond them in his own talks. The Resurrection of Jesus; the work of the

Holy Spirit; the Sacraments of the Church; these were subjects he would discuss, but rarely gave prominence in his teaching – nothing must detract from the wonderful simplicity of the heart of the Christian gospel.

A speaker, then, who sees his message in such blindingly simple terms begins with a great advantage – he is unlikely to be sidetracked into what he might see as irrelevancies and what his audience might find distracting. His task is to commend the teaching with all the clarity and vividness at his command. And most who heard Bash will associate his method with the memorable 'A,B,C' approach. First, he would say, we must Admit our need; and he would remind us of the Bible claim that Man is a fallen creature. This truth he would see as self-evident, not only in human history and the current world-scene but also in the instincts and daily experience of his hearers. And as he candidly laid his argument before us, many of us acknowledged the echo in our own hearts that – in St Paul's words, which he loved to quote – 'all have sinned and come short of the glory of God'. He loved alliteration, and would remind us how sin spoils God's fair creation and our own lives; how it makes slaves of those who yield with habits so hard to break; how it separates a man from the presence of a loving God – effectively in this life and finally in eternity.

Next, we must Believe that Christ died for us. And then he loved to go on to describe God's remedy – the coming of Jesus in the incarnation out of love for rebellious man; the perfect life lived out on earth as a demonstration of what God intended human life to be; the betrayal and mockery of a trial and all the horror of the passion, culminating (as he saw it) in the cry of dereliction at Calvary 'My God, my God, why hast *Thou* forsaken me?'. Those who heard Bash speaking of the cross will never forget his graphic, alarmingly simple, illustration of how God 'Laid man's sins on Jesus'. In his right hand he would take his small, well-worn, pocket Bible – 'this black thing'. Then, extending his left hand, he would slowly rotate the Bible on to the left hand from the right, reciting the while from his beloved Isaiah fifty-three 'the Lord laid on him the iniquity of us all'. 'Where are *your* sins?' he would add – 'on yourself, or on Jesus?'. And he might well clinch his argument with a favourite quotation from the 1662 Communion Service (the loss of which made him suspicious of Series Three:) – 'He made there by his one oblation of himself once offered a full perfect and sufficient sacrifice oblation and satisfaction for the sins of the whole world'.

It is not difficult to dismiss such an account as naive; and of course it does little justice to the notorious complexity of the doctrine of Original Sin and the Atonement; yet to hear what is, after all, the essence of the matter for Christian believers proclaimed with such clarity and sincerity – without a hint of deliberate emotionalism or of playing for effect – was to be captivated and, in many cases, to be won for a lifetime devoted to proclamation of the same gospel.

A; B; what is left for C? C is for Come. He would go on to explain – again in crystal clear language – how the remedy God has provided for sin is available for all who will personally accept it. Faith, in fact, is the act of inviting this Jesus of Calvary into the individual life. Once admitted, Jesus will cleanse from past sin, lend us his own strength to deal with present temptation, and – as long as we obey him – guide and direct the future. He will come as Saviour, Friend and Master; and we may rest assured that he will never leave us. Then he would turn in his worn bible to Revelation 3.20 ('This page,' he would add with a twinkle, 'is almost falling out') – 'Behold I stand at the door and knock . . . if any man . . . open the door, *I will come in*'. Holman Hunt's picture of 'The Light of the World' would be described, sometimes a reproduction held up. The hearers would be left confronted with the challenge – 'Will you . . . open the door?'

Of course there were many other talks, variations on the theme; but it was undoubtedly this particular address which most will remember, and which for many will encapsulate the essential 'Bash' message. Irreverent friends of his love to recount how, over a cup of tea immediately before he was due to address a crowd of undergraduates, he was hear to say he needed a moment to prepare. He then scrawled a few words on the back of an envelope; and when a curious observer later inspected the 'sermon-notes', he found they ran – 'Christianity: historical, institutional, personal, A B C: Rev. 3.20'.

Then, authority. To quote again an appraisal of our Lord – 'He taught as one having authority, not as the scribes'. Bash, like his Master, saw little need to rant and tub-thump, he was so confident that his words would carry their own conviction that he had no need to use such devices. As a realist, too, he knew full well that there is little value in a 'decision' made in an emotive atmosphere at a service or meeting; he much preferred to commend his message to the conscience and reason of a man, as well as to his emotions. Not that he was in any doubt, or left the hearer in any doubt, that the issue was urgent or vitally important – the right decision now might well change the whole course of a life (indeed of a destiny), and so it was far better taken quietly and thoughtfully, away from the crowds. In discussing this aspect of his preaching – and helping others too with their own approach – he could be deliberately dampening to the enthusiast who might be tempted to use extravagant language. 'You say he was "converted" last night? Well, say "professed conversion"'. 'Pray not for eloquence, but for utterance (as in Ephesians 6.19 – A.V.of course!)' And one public school chaplain claims to have treasured for many years a note passed to him a few moments before he stood up to give an address. It read, succinctly but disconcertingly, 'Be winsome . . . genial . . . gracious . . . engaging . . . clear-cut, logical . . . doctrinal . . . not too fast.' Rather a tall order, one might suppose – especially when there is minimal time to adjust to the required pattern. But at least it summarises the model upon which Bash – who of course had scrawled and passed the note – based his own practice. His words went home because they came from a man who was sure of his ground and had no need to bolster his assurance with bombast.

Nothing has been said – except in passing – about one feature of the talks which will be long remembered – the introduction of illustrations. He was not, in fact, a great concocter of complicated analogies (though he gave unstinted praise to friends who were), and his illustrations were distinctly traditional in type. He loved to take one of the Old Testament stories to illustrate God's power to heal and protect – the Passover, the Brazen Serpent, Naaman the leper – and to allow his imagination to play upon the details. He liked to regale hearers with details of his domestic arrangements (his aunt's numerous cats were a favourite theme); he introduced anecdotes which must have originated in books of Victorian sermons (the stage-coachman in his delirium – 'I'm going downhill, and I can't find the brake'.) But though we smiled – sometimes laughed uncontrollably – at the whimsical touches (the Israelite child's wrist-watch; the maid who looked after Mrs Naaman's dressing table), we never did so in disdain. These stories – though we ourselves could never have told them in quite his way – were an endearing feature of the man we so respected and loved.

Like many others who have become effective and attractive

speakers as they grow older, Bash owed much to his early experience amongst children. Those who heard his talks at the camps for 'slum boys' which he used to run before the war, or at parochial and seaside missions for children, will remember the simplicity, the economy of words and the winsome, almost playful sense of humour which made them so appealing. Like so many who have worked for Scripture Union, Bash admitted his indebtedness to Dick Hudson Pope, that prince of children's evangelists, whom he so greatly admired. 'RHP' (as he was always known) demonstrated that what children needed and welcomed were not little moral 'pep-talks', but solid Christian truth, made palatable and digestible by simple presentation, a wealth of illustration (very often with a visual-aid) and a delicate lightness of touch. It was qualities such as these, adapted to the needs of the teenager or university student, which helped to make Bash such a compelling and penetrating speaker.

Nothing approaching justice has been done in these short paragraphs. There have been – and still are – many preachers of far greater eloquence; some, of us question whether there have been many whose influence – through talks as well as through life – has been so powerful and so lasting. 'We shall not look upon his like again'.

6: The Counsellor and friend

John Stott

From 1940-45 John Stott worked very closely with Bash as Secretary and Treasurer of the camps. In 1945 he was ordained to a curacy at All Souls, Langham Place, and became Rector of the parish in 1950. He is now Rector Emeritus, and though still based in London, he exercises a world-wide ministry, and is also the author of a large number of books.

6: The counsellor and friend

When Hugh Lyon was headmaster of Rugby School, he often used the expression which Alexander Pope coined towards the end of his *Essay on Man:* a 'guide, philosopher and friend'. Each of us needed one, he would say, and should seek to be one to others. It is certainly what Bash was to me during a particularly formative period of my life, as he was to countless other boys, undergraduates and young professional men.

My adolescence was typically religious. Though my father, a physician, was a scientific secularist, my mother had been brought up as a devout Lutheran. She taught my sisters and me to go to church on Sundays, and to read the Bible and 'say our prayers' daily, which practice I continued throughout my early teens, more out of affectionate loyalty to her and out of routine, than as a personally meaningful discipline. In fact, I found the whole exercise extremely unsatisfying. Convinced that there was more to religion than I had so far discovered, I used on half holiday afternoons to creep into the Memorial Chapel by myself, in order to read religious books, absorb the atmosphere of mystery, and seek for God. But he continued to elude me.

It was John Bridger, one year ahead of me in the Modern Languages department, who invited me to attend what today would be called the 'Christian Union'. It had no name then and was usually referred to anonymously as 'the meeting', though in my diary I called it rather disrespectfully 'Bridger's Affair'. I continued attending it every Sunday afternoon for several months until a memorable day in February 1938 on which, it was announced, there would be a visiting speaker named the Reverend E.J.H. Nash. He was nothing much to look at, and certainly no ambassador for muscular Christianity. Yet as he spoke I was riveted. His text was Pilate's question: 'What then shall I do with Jesus, who is called the Christ?'. That I needed to *do* anything with Jesus was an entirely novel idea to me, for I had imagined that somehow he had done whatever needed to be done, and that my part was only to acquiesce. This Mr

Nash, however, was quietly but powerfully insisting that everybody had to do something about Jesus, and that nobody could remain neutral. Either we copy Pilate and weakly reject him, or we accept him personally and follow him.

When the meeting was over, I went up to ask our visiting speaker some questions, the nature of which I do not now recall. What I do remember is that he had the spiritual discernment to recognise in me a seeking soul. So he took me for a drive in his car, answered my questions and explained to me the way of salvation. To my astonishment his presentation of Christ crucified and risen exactly corresponded with the needs of which I was aware. But he exerted no pressure upon me. He had the sensitivity and wisdom to let me go, so that I could 'open the door' to Christ by myself, which I did that very night by my bedside in the dormitory, while the other boys were in bed and asleep.

A few days later his first letter arrived, enclosing a booklet and giving practical advice on how to go on and grow as a Christian. A correspondence then developed between us, and he must have written to me once a week for at least five years. I still marvel at his faithfulness. For often they were long letters, broken into paragraphs with sectional headings underlined. Some paragraphs were heavily theological, unfolding the doctrine of the Atonement or the three tenses of salvation. Others were ethical, expounding the principles of moral conduct or marshalling the arguments – a bit too rigidly, as I now believe – why a certain practice should be regarded as 'worldly' and therefore avoided. Other paragraphs contained pastoral guidance on how to read the Bible, how to pray, or how to practise the presence of Christ each day so that he became as real on the rugger field as in chapel. In yet other paragraphs he would give detailed advice on how to run the Sunday meeting (whose leadership I took over from John Bridger when he went up to Cambridge), how to help other boys who were young in their faith, and how to recruit for the holiday camps. There was personal counsel too, especially on the need to get ten hours' sleep every night. Then every letter would end with a 'best thought', some precious biblical text opened up and applied. Alongside the best thought, however, often as a postscript and perhaps always as a deliberate prophylactic against an excess of piety, he would add a joke, usually of the schoolboy howler variety.

I do not know any Christian leader of modern days who shared, as he did, the apostle Paul's conviction about the value of letter-writing. Bash was never separated from his writing materials, especially on his 'missionary journeys'. During the war he continued to travel, sometimes driving many miles to visit a small group or even only one boy, or using the erratic wartime train service. One of my most characteristic memories of him is to see him on an ill-lit railway platform during the blackout, with his attaché case on his knees and his writing pad on it, 'redeeming the time' by writing letters.

When the war broke out I was a very immature Christian, barely eighteen months old, and would describe myself as an instinctive pacifist. I had now read the Sermon on the Mount for the first time, with its commands not to resist evil but rather to turn the other cheek and to love our enemies. It seemed to me impossible to reconcile these injunctions with war. Nobody introduced me to the 'just war' theory or helped me to balance the biblical arguments. Bash was a pacifist himself, more perhaps on pragmatic than on clear doctrinal grounds, but he was no propagandist and did nothing to influence me. In fact, I mention my own pacifism only because of its effect on my relations with my family and therefore with Bash. My father became a Major-General in the Army Medical Service, and understandably could not come to terms with having a son who was a conscientious objector (although as an ordinand I was given exemption from military service and never needed to go before a tribunal). For about two years he found it virtually impossible to speak to me, and could not make up his mind whether he could continue to support me at Cambridge. Since we were a very united and affectionate family, we all found those years extremely painful. It was because of this alienation from my father that Bash became almost a surrogate father to me. He was very sympathetic towards me in my dilemma. At the same time, he was never weak or sentimental. His expectations for all those whom he led to Christ were extremely high. He could be easily disappointed. His letters to me often contained rebuke, for I was a wayward young Christian and needed to be disciplined. In fact, so frequent were his admonitions at one period that, whenever I saw his familiar writing on an envelope, I needed to pray and prepare myself for half an hour before I felt ready to open it.

Bash could be a ruthless critic. He seemed to have no fear of losing a person's respect or friendship. If a clear doctrinal or moral principle was at stake, he was fearlessly outspoken. He did not know how to beat about the bush. He went straight to the point. 'Faithful are the wounds of a friend', he would quote, and again 'the fear of man brings a snare'.

Nothing seemed to exasperate him more than humbug. It was impossible to deceive him. He saw straight through all attempts to do so. Pomposity was as obnoxious to him as hypocrisy. I think that was why he sometimes allowed his humour to run away with him. He could be merciless in pulling somebody's leg. Whether consciously or not, it was the weapon he used to undermine a person who took himself too seriously. 'It humbles him, man'. Paradoxically, I think he used flattery for the same ultimate purpose. It was so outrageous as to be a self-evident kind of mockery. Woe betide the person who thought it was serious and accepted the praise; his vanity was quickly exposed. Yet neither his teasing nor his flattering was ever malicious. He was a deeply humble and unassuming man himself. Like his Master, he hated pride and knew that everything which promoted humility in people was to their own advantage and blessing.

Humility to Bash was synonymous with dependence. He told me several times of the serious illness he had had when he was a young man. When he was at his lowest ebb, and was not at all sure that he would survive, he remembered being so helpless that he needed to be fed. This utter dependence which in a sense was for him the ultimate in humiliation, seems also to have been the beginning of humility. He learned then the inescapable fact of our human dependence on each other, and even more on God. The humility of a little child, to which Jesus several times alluded, is the humility of dependence. It is right to refer to children as 'dependants', for that is what they are, dependent on their parents for everything they possess. It was thus that Bash thought of himself before God. Although his gospel focused almost exclusively on Jesus – the Saviour, the Lord and the Friend – yet in his own devotional life the Fatherhood of God meant much to him. He would often refer to Hudson Taylor in this connection. 'I am a bad father', Hudson Taylor would say, 'but it is not my habit to forget my children; God is a very, very good Father; it is not his habit to forget his children'.

Such humble dependence on God the Father naturally expressed itself in prayer. And Bash was a mighty – if unorthodox – man of prayer. If one's vision of the prayer warrior is of a saint who gets up at four in the morning, Bash does not fit this stereotype at all. Convinced of the primary importance of having adequate sleep, he had no intention of getting up early. Yet he would often be awake early, and both then and during his afternoon siesta, he would lie on his back, with a handkerchief over his eyes to keep out the distractions of the light, and he would be praying. He had a long intercessory prayer list, and his persevering faithfulness in using it constantly put me to shame. When praying with one person, or taking part in a prayer meeting, one knew that long experience had accustomed him to converse with God. His voice was matter-of-fact, his language down-to-earth, and his goal to see Satan bound and God liberated to do his will and finish his work. He had definite expectations that prayer would work, or rather that God would work in answer to prayer.

Another mark of his humility was his ability to delegate, and the high degree of confidence he placed in those to whom he entrusted responsibility. He did not surround himself with nonentities, as small men do, in order that their own leadership is not threatened. On the contrary, the camp officers he appointed were often more gifted than he in either intellectual calibre or athletic prowess or both. He was content to take a back seat personally, and to let them hold the floor and receive the kudos. I never detected in him even the slightest tinge of jealousy. On the contrary, so anxious was he to bring others forward and see them develop, that he took extraordinary risks and gave some people responsibilities which were well beyond their years, their experience and their capacity. I was myself still at school when he invited me to join his team in the children's beach mission at Borth in mid-Wales and later to share with him in a mission in a Free Church in the country. And I was a freshman at university when he first entrusted me with the privilege of giving the Sunday afternoon 'Bible Reading' to senior boys at camp. Though I blush when I remember some of the naive and even downright erroneous notions I taught, I can never be thankful enough that Bash pushed me into the deep end to sink or swim.

Greatly tempted to discouragement himself, he went out of his way to encourage others, especially young men at the threshold of their ministry. If 'Love has great expectations' (1 Cor. 13:7), then Bash loved much, for he expected much from even his most junior colleagues. Moreover, however much one floundered, he was nearly always generous in his words of appreciation, although bold in constructive criticism when the situation demanded it.

Behind and beneath the practical policies which he developed, there was an unshakeable conviction that God had called him. Though himself the son of a clergyman and brought up in a godly home, he still needed – and in due course experienced – a personal encounter with Christ. It happened in a train in 1917, if I remember correctly, and it changed the course of his life. For he believed he had been called not only to belong to Christ but to serve him, and to serve him not just in general terms but in the very specific sphere of Britain's (indeed largely England's) leading boys' public schools. From that moment on he was determined to be obedient to the heavenly vision; nothing would deflect him from it. Indeed the criticisms which have been levelled against him can be met, and his eccentricities explained, only in the light of the particular call and commission he knew he had received.

The commonest criticism related to his concentration on the public schools, and on the top few at that. It was easy to dismiss him as an élitist or a snob. But people who thought and talked that way simply did not understand Bash. What motivated him was not snobbery, but strategy. He believed that God had called him to work in these schools, and that the reason for this divine call was that the future leadership of church and state was to be found there. He was entirely consistent, moreover, in working this out. 'Shorts of three kinds will be worn' was the peremptory pre-camp instruction. It was much ridiculed, but the logic was to make boys feel at home among people who dressed alike. The fact was that white, grey or navy-blue shorts were then the convention at public schools, while khaki was frowned on. The same principle applied in all Bash's apparently pernickety regulations about where to part your hair, how to begin and end letters, and how not to clip your pens and pencils to your outside pocket. It was a matter of decorum, of following the strict code of what was 'done' and 'not done' in public schools between the wars. There was certainly snobbery in the schools during that period; Bash conformed at camp only for the sake of the gospel. The gospel had a big enough 'scandal' of its own; there was no point in adding to it unnecessary cultural stumbling blocks.

Bash's health fads were another aspect of his sense of call. Unfriendly critics will say that he suffered from a mild hypochondria, imagining illnesses he did not have, and prescribing for himself (or persuading his doctors to prescribe for him) innumerable, unnecessary remedies. The pills and lozenges, lotions and potions which accompanied him everywhere were a wonder to behold. His friends all got to know his fears of infection (through drinking out of a café's 'buggy' cup), his predilections for some foods (e.g. cucumber, brown bread, marmalade, eggs and bacon) and his avoidance of others (especially everything even remotely 'pippy'). We laughed and teased him. He, on the other hand, did more than rationalize his habits; he actually theologized them. 'You are not your own', he would quote, 'for you were bought with a price' and 'your body is a temple of the Holy Spirit'. Therefore, he would add, you have no right to neglect your bodies. On the contrary, you must 'glorify God in your bodies' and take good care of them. He had a genuine concern for the health of his officers, not just for his own. Unashamedly, he wanted to live a long life, not in order to retire (he never did) but in order to have more time in which to serve Christ and win souls. He was not ignorant of Satan's devices, and was determined to thwart him in his undoubted desire to bump Christ's servants off prematurely.

As with health, so with humour. Bash loved the kind of calendar which had a daily tear-off slip, and it is difficult to say whether he preferred the 'best thought' or the joke variety. The torn-off jokes he would carry about in his wallet and produce at embarrassing moments, with twinkling eyes and an enquiring 'do you know this one, man?' Some of the jokes can only be described as puerile. So was he just an immature schoolboy, who had never grown up? Doubtless his detractors would say so. But I dissent. It was partly an innocent sense of fun. It also had theological overtones, however. For schoolboy humour was a way into the schoolboy heart. He both admired and imitated Paul's resolve to be 'all things to all men', in order to win them. He thought childlike humour good for adults, too. It was effective in pricking their pompous bubbles and in relaxing them when they became too tense. He hated religious intensity and hothouse fervour, believing them to be unnatural. Humour was his weapon of counterattack. When the Scripture Union Council entertained fears that Bash was exerting an 'undue influence' on the boys who came to his camps, Dr John Laird, the SU General Secretary, went down to Iwerne Minster to see for himself. 'My fears were dispersed like the mist', he recently told me, 'when I saw the quality of men he had gathered round him, and the openness, freedom and genuineness of the atmosphere'.

Bash's sense of call also accounted for his attitude to World War II. I was at Beachborough as a camper just before it broke out. Not long afterwards, we were sitting together in his famous Rover car, talking. He was deeply disturbed by the outbreak of hostilities. We read from Matthew 24 'you will hear of wars and rumours of wars; see that you are not troubled'. It seemed to be a word from God himself, that even a major world war was not going to be permitted to disrupt his work through camp. 'Bust Hitler' he would say, when some wartime shortage or other frustration threatened to disrupt camp. It would be easy for unsympathetic critics to condemn this attitude as extremely narrowminded and self-centred, when the survival of freedom itself was at stake. Yet, it was perfectly consistent. Bash was not insensitive to the horrors of the war. He grieved deeply when names of campers and officers appeared on the casualty lists. He also followed the course of the battles being fought, with the aid of the dramatic diagrams in his Daily Mail. Yet he knew he was engaged in another and even more serious battle, whose outcome would settle people's eternal destinies. Who can gainsay the truth of his perspective?

This brings me to the subject for which Bash has been most severely criticized, namely his attitude to marriage. He was accused of grave imbalance, of an unhealthy policy of dissuading his officers from marrying, and even (it was sometimes darkly hinted) of latent homosexual tendencies. Since I worked with him closely for about seven years, both as a personal friend and as camp's secretary-treasurer, I am able to say with complete confidence that Bash was a perfectly normal heterosexual. His own singleness, and his advocacy of the single state, were entirely due to his zeal for God's work. He took 1 Corinthians 7 seriously and had the courage (which few have) to quote it approvingly. He also quoted Jesus to the effect that 'there are eunuchs who have made themselves eunuchs for the sake of the kingdom of heaven' (Matt 19:12). He was one such himself – not of course literally (as in the case of Origen's misguided self-mutilation) but figuratively, choosing deliberately to remain single for the sake of God's kingdom. He may sometimes have been too zealous in commending singleness to others, assuming too readily that they also had received this particular gift and calling, but I for one greatly admire his courage and faithfulness in facing issues which many of us shirk. He cultivated a ruthless self-discipline himself in the fight against temptation, and urged upon others the same safeguards and self-control. He was adamant that Christians are at liberty to marry only Christians, and indeed that mature Christians should marry only mature Christians, so that they may help rather than hinder one another in their Christian life and service. He boldly confronted and rebuked officers who became involved with an unbelieving or otherwise unsuitable girl, and pleaded with them to draw back before it was too late. Many an officer tremblingly brought his girlfriend or fiancée to Bash to be vetted. Understandably, it raises a smile. But I know no Christian leader who has acted as consistently as Bash in applying the Pauline teaching that those who are chosen for pastoral oversight must have a blameless reputation in sex, marriage and home (1 Tim. 3.2-5; Tit. 1.6,7).

The phrase which best sums up what I have been trying to emphasize is Paul's (for whom Bash had a special predilection) in Phil. 3.13 (RSV). 'One thing I do, forgetting what lies behind and straining forward to what lies ahead, I press on towards the goal. . .'. Bash was a man of 'one thing'. He had seen Jesus and heard his call. Nothing was permitted to distract him from it. All deviations were diabolical. One of his greatest heroes was D.L. Moody, and one of his favourite books R.A. Torrey's *Why God used D.L. Moody.* Of the seven reasons Torrey gave, perhaps the most important was that God had all there was of Moody to have. God had all there was of Bash also. He was neither a platform man nor a pulpiteer. He shunned publicity, lest he should call attention to himself. 'His charm', wrote David C.C. Watson (formerly of the Dohnavur Fellowship, South India) in a private letter, 'drew one only to Christ, not to himself'. It is true. Non-descript in outward appearance, his heart was ablaze with Christ. Conscientiously self-effacing, his whole life bore witness to Christ. One could wish for no greater quality than Christlikeness in a 'guide, philosopher and friend'.

7: The leader

Ian Dobbie

Colonel Dobbie is a regular army officer, a Sapper, who was trained at Sandhurst and later at Shrivenham, at the Royal Military College of Science. He has served in many parts of the world, and in this country has had much to do with house parties in connexion with Officers' Christian Union. He is a grandson of Lieut.-General Sir William Dobbie, the war-time Governor-General of 'Malta GC'.

7: The leader

Near the centre of Aldershot stands the 'Miss Daniell's Soldiers' Home', a centre of Christian endeavour founded by a Victorian evangelical lady. Bash used to make use of this home occasionally during the days of National Service, when he would take out one of his campers for a meal and a short time of Bible-reading and prayer together. It was the Lady Superintendent of this home who once gave a succinct definition of a leader – 'Someone who has a following'.

Bash was someone who had a following, for as one diocesan Bishop said of him: 'He has done more to change the face of the Church of England than anyone else this century'. And yet my early memories of him, even allowing for the limited powers of my youthful judgement, would not have suggested that he would make so impressive an impact; but at human level God gave him *influence* which, as is so often the case, was to be more important than power.

Bash used to speak annually in chapel at my preparatory school. I can only recall one part of those addresses. Bash reminded us that in the trench warfare of World War 1 it was not easy to keep in touch with headquarters, and indeed it was all too easy to get cut off. He drew spiritual parallel of the importance of the Christian maintaining communications with his heavenly Father through Bible-reading and prayer, a theme I was to hear him reiterate no doubt many times in later years.

Bash was a meek man but there was a ring of divine authority about him. This made me want to sit at his feet when several years later I heard him speak at Iwerne Minster and at the school meeting at Wellington; for intuitively I sensed that he was a man who knew God, was confident about that relationship and longed that others should be also. At that stage in my spiritual pilgrimage I was glad to be led by such a man and, although my opportunities to meet him over the years were limited by professional and other spiritual commitments, that willingness never diminished.

At first sight, however, Bash would not have appeared as an

obvious candidate for leadership in the mission field to which his God has appointed him. There was no masculine panache; in an age in which the gladiator was revered, he was untalented at games; and in his early life his acquaintance with the English public school system was limited. But the Master he served has a sovereign way of fashioning men from unlikely material, lest any man should glory in the flesh. He rejoices to make 'his strength perfect in weakness' and he did this with Bash.

Field-Marshal Montgomery reckoned there were seven key ingredients necessary in a successful leader in war, and all of them are applicable to spiritual warfare as well. The leader must:

1. Be able to sit back and avoid getting immersed in detail.
2. Not be petty.
3. Not be pompous.
4. Be a good picker of men.
5. Trust those under him and let them get on with their job without interference.
6. Possess the power of clear decision.
7. Inspire confidence.

Bash had all these gifts; but he had others also which major on the spiritual dimension, including the most crucial of all; for he himself had learnt to be led and to obey. He had taken seriously the command of Jesus, the Supreme Commander to follow him and to be made 'a fisher of men'. By following and obeying him day by day the foundation was laid on which other spiritual qualities could rest and flourish.

No one would question that the Lord placed a remarkable singleness of mind and purpose in Bash. It was to prove of paramount importance. With Bash it was 'one thing I know' and like the Apostle Paul, 'one thing I do'. No one who worked under him could doubt what was required of him. We were all expected to be involved in the great work of serving God. Everthing was to be subordinate to this; for he believed that the Lord had 'raised up camp for a definite purpose', and we must do nothing to frustrate that plan. Armed with this glorious and consuming obsession, Bash made life for himself as a leader very much easier. Communication became simpler than might have been expected. Subordinates found it difficult to disobey an order; for not only was the aim noble beyond compare, but also we knew that Bash would never ask us to do something he would not be willing to do himself. Like the true leader he was, he was prepared to suffer for the sake of his Master and the objectives he had been given.

Bash would doubtless have agreed with the great Salvation Army worker, Samuel Logan Brengle, who outlined the road to spiritual authority and leadership in challenging words:

> 'It is not won by promotion but by many prayers and tears. It is attained by confessions of sin, and much heartsearching and humbling before God; by self-surrender, a courageous sacrifice of every idol, a bold deathless uncompromising and uncomplaining embracing of the cross, and by an eternal, unfaltering looking unto Jesus crucified. It is not gained by seeking great things for ourselves, but rather like Paul, by counting those things that are gain to us as loss for Christ. That is a great price, but it must be unflinchingly paid by him who would not be merely a nominal but a real spiritual leader of men, a leader whose power is recognised and felt in heaven, on earth and in hell'.[1]

If however Bash's singlemindedness was costly to himself, it was also inspiring to others. Without great conscious effort he seemed to sway men, who instinctively followed and trusted him. As someone said of Pastor Hsi, so of Bash it could be said also: 'One could not be with him without gaining a wholly new ideal of Christian life and service'.

This unswerving singlemindedness also made it easier for Bash to select his lieutenants. He knew what he was looking for. Like Cromwell of old, 'he would rather have a russet-coated captain who knows what he believes and believes what he knows'. This was reflected in the men he picked to work with him on the camp staff and in his choice of a successor. It was said of the well known Methodist Dr W.E. Sangster that 'his greatest grasp of leadership was knowing the importance of delegation and of choosing assistants with care'.[2] Bash was given this talent also. This ability to pick subordinates was clearly critical to a man of his limited range of

[1] S.L. Brengle *The Soul Winner's Secret* p22
[2] Paul Sangster *Doctor Sangster* p221

natural talents. Besides, the Iwerne Minster camp machine became too large for continuous personal leadership to be exercised in all areas, and delegation became essential. But he did more than delegate, for he came to depend to a remarkable degree upon those to whom he entrusted some of the 'diplomatic' and administrative aspects of his work, accepting their advice and rarely questioning their judgement. When such complete confidence is reposed in subordinates, and they are encouraged to work without interference and even supervision, it brings out the very best in them, and they respond with the loyalty and devotion which such a generous attitude deserves.

In training his subordinates Bash did not flinch from adopting tactics which are not universally popular in our modern secular world, nor in Christian circles to-day. He believed in exploiting success rather than reinforcing failure. Bash was prepared to leave on one side men who lacked fibre or commitment. Shallowness had to be eliminated. Nor was any man immune from receiving a well-earned rebuke. Indeed a Christian Lieutenant Colonel assured me a few years ago that the biggest 'rocket' he had ever received was from Mr Nash. Knowing what a lively subaltern he had been, and that he would have received his full ration from his military masters, I realised that Bash would have given him nothing less than 'the full treatment'. He realised that he had deserved the lash and so did not resent it. On the contrary it made him regard Bash with an even greater respect than before.

In the Sermon on the Mount Jesus told us not only to move the plank from our own eye, but also to remove the splinter from our brother's. Bash took that command seriously. Rebukes were not limited to the spoken word on a private occasion. The man who failed to speak up at the prayer meeting or who made an inane comment in an officer's meeting was liable to receive a broadside without delay, not to humiliate him but so that all of us might learn together. Letters postmarked Maidenhead were known to be opened with trepidation even by Bishops and principals of Theological Colleges.

But it would be a very grave mistake to suggest that such high standards were secured by fierce, Prussian discipline. On the contrary he knew how to encourage and draw alongside men. He rejoiced at their successes and knew when to give praise where it was due, and never failed to express his appreciation and delight to those who had earned it. Friendship of a most caring sort was a distinct mark of Bash's leadership. King David in the Old Testament was able so to capture men's allegiance and affection that a wish would be translated into a command, (2 Sam. 23:15-16); and Bash had the same sort of ability to gather round him men of considerable talent, and in a totally unemotional way to nurture them.

Someone once said that Bash had an almost feminine gift of intuition which enabled him to perceive one's need and to give the appropriate help or advice. His knowledge of Scripture was so comprehensive that he could trust the Holy Spirit to take him to just the right verse to pass on to a man or boy and so release him from a problem. He knew his Master had declared that truth would make men free and that his word was truth and, believing this, he applied it diligently.

Few men since apostolic times have covered their converts so faithfully in prayer and with letters of encouragement. The ministry of Bash's pen was mighty. John Stott pays special tribute to this in his book *Guard the Gospel,* and elsewhere in this volume. It was thus not difficult to confide in him on the most personal matters and one of the abiding reflections many will have retained is Bash's absence of surprise as problems were aired. His experience and purity of motive made his leadership at this personal level something to be valued and cherished.

If however, Bash's singlemindedness was especially evident in his leadership, the simplicity of his gospel was not a jot the less so. Scripture declared this gospel to be 'Tidings of Great Joy' and he determined to represent it in that light. This did not make him flinch from speaking decisively about sin and its consequences, but he rejoiced to match it with the good news that Jesus Christ, the Friend of sinners, could release us from that guilt and bondage. Literally hundreds of boys and young men had cause to be eternally grateful for this unspeakably wonderful message proclaimed with artless simplicity and love. Compared with the formality and implied necessity to earn one's salvation, delivered with unrelenting aridity in so many churches and schools, this was a gospel with a ring of truth, joy and authority. It was attractive; it was to be seized without delay. It provided a wiping away of failure and shameful past performance and a strong confidence for the future. Supremely, this brand of Christianity was biblical, authentic and orthodox. There was nothing counterfeit. It was unemotional, unsensational and yet practical. It made coming to faith in Jesus Christ a sensible and almost natural thing to do. It made the Saviour a living Person whose friendship could be experienced day by day.

Some have suggested that this gospel was too simple and that Bash appeared to despise scholarship. This criticism may be answered in two ways. First those he led were generally satisfied with the range of intellectual content provided for as long as they were directly under Bash's leadership. As men grew older and their ministry took them to places which contained a more intellectual challenge, they had cause to be grateful to Bash for laying so firm a Biblical foundation to their faith. As Dr Oliver Barclay has written, Bash's men were 'reliable in policy and doctrine' and that in their generation 'the ablest men became intellectually and theologically some of the more adventurous and effective evangelists and teachers'.[3] Secondly it must be remembered that Bash himself emerged in an age when evangelical scholarship was relatively scarce. He and men of his generation had to hold on in faith to the foundation truths that Scripture provided. They honoured God and he honoured their ministry.

This simplicity of belief was not only purveyed in camp talks and school meetings. It was evident on car journeys and on visits to his home at 10, Crauford Rise. No opportunity was lost to send forth something of the 'simplicity that is in Christ Jesus'. It was apparent also in Bash's leadership of Prayers and his officers' meetings. The singing of choruses, intercessions and readings from Scripture were not allowed to be treated in a perfunctory manner. Key aspects of the gospel would be brought forth from a line in a hymn or chorus, supported by some apposite comment or illustration, and the chorus then sung a second time. All this was designed to provide an introduction to the truth to be expounded in the talk that followed. Nothing was to be done without aim or purpose. Bash fervently advocated basing extempore prayer on a verse of Scripture, whether for praise or intercession. In this way he believed the Christian did business with his heavenly Father on ground which God himself had chosen and promised to bless already; and he led by example. The last prayer I heard him pray on a visit to him was introduced with 'Seek ye my face . . . thy face Lord will I seek'.

Bash was keenly aware of the importance of his officers' meetings

[3] Oliver R. Barclay *Whatever happened to the Jesus Lane lot?* p105, 106

as a vehicle for the training of his team. He achieved a remarkable blend of democracy and autocracy in leading them. Too much democracy would have meant that the work at Iwerne Minster lacked the direction and wisdom which were founded upon experience; too much autocracy on the other hand, would have stifled the creative instincts and confidence of younger men and led to a work impoverished of a dynamic influence. Even the youngest was encouraged to contribute, knowing that Bash himself would unhesitatingly overrule if wisdom required it. The need for this wisdom which is given such prominence in the New Testament in the selection of subordinate leaders, where we read that the first deacons were required to be 'of honest report, full of the Holy Ghost and wisdom', always included courtesy and loyalty to school authorities. It may not have been an easy lesson for a man with such strong convictions as Bash to learn, but learn it he did, and the work of camp blossomed and prospered as it gained the confidence of an increasing number of school-masters and chaplains, because like David of old its representatives 'behaved themselves wisely'.

Bash knew that seasoned leadership must appeal to heart and mind. He knew also that a leader does not inspire his followers if he is unbusinesslike. His work therefore in every respect was systematic and methodical. He never went into battle without a proper plan. Yet in spite of this controlled efficiency he was a relaxed character. Furthermore he wanted others to relax also. He sought to protect camp from becoming too busy or hectic, for he saw that officers and boys would find it spiritually barren if it became so. Although he disliked heartiness, and I doubt whether I ever heard him guffaw or giggle, he delighted in a good anecdote or joke preferably from a raconteur who did not laugh at his own humour. He liked the boys to laugh also, especially in a work where many would be counting the cost in the weighty matters of sin and salvation. He never wanted to see young people under strain and he felt that well timed and appropriate humour would deliver camp from any fear of intensity.

An over enthusiastic young officer once admonished Bash about the consumption of chocolate at camp during the war years. He fervently pleaded for this luxury to be set aside for refugees. This sort of intense zeal was more than Bash could stomach. 'Oh shut up, John' he retorted, 'you'll go batty!'

It is perhaps one mark of a great leader that he becomes a legend in his own life time, and stories and anecdotes collect round him, some true, others exaggerated and others again completely fabricated. Bash was no exception, and wherever his friends and followers gathered, they would regale each other with reminiscences, each one probably a little more irreverent and apochryphal than the last. But somehow this could all be done without in anyway undermining the loyalty, affection and respect with which he was regarded, and if these tales were repeated to Bash himself, he would enjoy them as much as anyone, for he was the least pompous of men, and could always laugh at himself.

Were there no limitations or shortcomings in Bash's leadership? I confess to being an unquestioning admirer. Some have suggested that he failed to relax his influence over men as they grew older. Perhaps this was so, but if it was a fault it was an understandable one. He was aware that men involved in careers, whether ecclesiastical or secular, could lose their first love for Jesus Christ. Singlemindedness and love of the simple gospel are not easily retained, and Bash knew it well. He was well acquainted with the Parable of the Sower, and he longed to keep his men from becoming unfruitful. He wanted to see every true Christian at his post fighting valiantly 'under Christ's banner as his faithful soldier and servant unto his life's end.' And so he would exhort, encourage and cajole us. Many will receive greater rewards in heaven as a result of Bash's promptings, even late in life, than if he had allowed them to pursue unprofitable courses unchallenged. Eternity will reveal that adherence to his counsel will have replaced 'wood, hay, stubble' with gold, silver, precious stones.

Bash's leadership was also criticised for being over selective and too specialised in its application. It was argued that his work was élitist in its aim for it concentrated on the privileged classes, on the potential leaders only and that they in their turn were encouraged to witness for Christ in that same limited field. Bash did not despise privilege, but hoped that those who enjoyed it would be suitably grateful, and mindful that it carried with it responsibilities. Had not the Master taught that 'unto whomsoever much is given, of him shall be much required'? And if the Public School system contained mischievous practices, were not these best attacked by proclaiming within these institutions the gospel of Christ? Moreover, the New Testament tells us that it is hard for the rich to enter the Kingdom of Heaven, which is a very good reason for concentrating missionary effort in their direction. Believing this to be so, Bash had no cause to repent of devoting his time to this missionfield.

He was sometimes criticised too for discouraging his men from seeking a ministry outside his own specialised field. But if this was his policy, it was singularly unsuccessful, as the following story will show. A few years ago an American post-graduate student was carrying out research for a thesis on Christian conversion. While attending a convention in Kenya he was apparently allowed to question a large group of men, hoping to detect some important influence which God had used to bring about their own conversions to Christ. He accordingly asked if anyone would be prepared to testify to any influence which had helped him.

'Well', began one man, 'I was converted at a place in Dorset, England called Iwerne Minster'. He continued and concluded his testimony.

'Yes', volunteered another man, 'funnily enough I was converted at Iwerne Minster also'.

'So was I', called out another.

'Me too', claimed another.

'Say,' remarked the American, 'how many of you guys were converted at this Iwerne Minster place?'

Here in the heart of Africa hands went up in all corners of the room. The American was duly impressed.

'Say, I guess I must send my kids to this place'.

A few years before Bash died, he was deeply touched to receive from Douglas Johnston, for many years a most distinguished and effective General Secretary of the I.V.F., a letter saying that wherever he travelled he noticed that he met men who had come to Christ at Iwerne Minster and that they were faithful husbandmen in their Master's vineyard.

My closing remarks relate to Bash's leadership as a speaker although this is covered more thoroughly elsewhere in this volume. Some years ago a number of Sandhurst instructors were discussing the key qualities needed by a leader. Several supported the view that ability to speak well was of unquestionable importance. In an artless but wonderfully powerful way, the Lord gave Bash that gift and it was through that gift that his leadership perhaps touched us most directly and effectively.

A few months ago as I attended Bash's funeral, I was profoundly moved as I heard 1 Corinthians 15 read. Bash had selected this passage himself.

'. . . I delivered to you as of first importance what I also received, that Christ died for our sins in accordance with the Scripture, that he was buried, that he was raised on the third day in accordance with the Scriptures . . . by the grace of God I am what I am, and his grace to me was not in vain. On the contrary, I worked harder than any of them, though it was not I, but the grace of God which is with me . . . so we preach and so you believed . . . Therefore, my beloved be steadfast, immovable always abounding in the work of the Lord, knowing that in the Lord your labour is not in vain?

I felt Bash had given his last talk that afternoon with all the singlemindedness and simplicity we were so often privileged to witness in his leadership. It will surely have rejoiced his Master's heart as much as it did our own.

8: The theologian

Michael Green

After several years as Principal of St John's College, Nottingham, Michael Green left to become Rector of St Aldate's, Oxford. He is the author of a number of widely read books, and as well as his work in Oxford, he has an extensive ministry as a preacher and lecturer in this country and overseas.

8: The theologian

Bash himself would have laughed at the title chosen for this chapter, for he never regarded himself in any sense of the word as a theologian. He knew no Hebrew and very little Greek, while his knowledge of the early fathers and church history was no more than was required to pass the fairly undemanding ordination examinations of the 1920's. When deep or abstruse questions arose in the course of discussion, he would invariably side-step them with some such comment as, 'We must ask Peter', or 'I wonder what Patrick would say'. In fact he often regarded theologians with suspicion and even mistrust. In his view too many of them knew all about the inner workings of the car, but had never learnt to drive it properly; for driving, to continue the metaphor, was the passion of Bash's life, and theology was only welcomed in so far as it ministered to that end.

There was too the genuine and understandable fear, felt not for himself but for others, especially his young converts, that too early and too radical an exposure to much that was being taught in the universities might undermine their faith before it was firmly established. It is true to say that as the climate of opinion began to change, and some leading theological thinkers took a more conservative turn, his views altered, his confidence grew and his fears subsided.

But of course, as he himself knew, theology is a subject which no Christian, let alone an ordained minister, can avoid. Every man must have his theology, that is to say, his understanding of the nature and character of God, and his own personal response to divinely revealed truths. No Christian worth his salt can fail to explore and investigate religious belief using the reason God has given him enlightened by faith (*fides quaerens intellectum*), and in this sense Bash was a theologian.

To what then did this investigation lead him? What were the ingredients of his faith? I think it is possible to isolate six distinct factors.

1. The sovereignty of God.

He was never heard to express the slightest doubt in the existence of an all-wise, -loving and -powerful Being for whose pleasure and purpose man was created, and in whose almighty providence man could rest in complete confidence and peace. And this God he always thought of quite naturally in two ways – as transcendent and immanent, or as he would have preferred to put it, 'in heaven' and 'at hand'.

You had only to hear him pray to realise the strength of his faith in this respect. He would speak to God as if he were in the same room with him, and yet he would attribute to this same intimate friend the power and wisdom which had created and now sustained the universe. It was this belief that encouraged him to pray about even the smallest details and circumstances of every day life; and having done so, to go to sleep with a newspaper over his face and leave the outcome with perfect contentment in the hands of God.

I think if he had been questioned more closely on this subject, he would probably have admitted that he saw prayer not so much as a series of specific requests for particular objects, but rather as an opportunity to make frequent use of the lines of communication between himself and God, and in this way to keep open and clean the channels through which God's power could flow into his own life and beyond.

Thus it never seemed to worry him unduly if his prayers appeared not to be answered in the way that he had hoped. If, for example, an earnest prayer for a fine day for some camp expedition or activity seemed to produce exactly the opposite result, he was perfectly happy to leave the final outcome in the providential hands of God, but knowing all the time that the prayer in the morning had been more than worth while, because it had deepened his intimacy with God and strengthened his dependence upon him.

Those who worked with him, or even observed him from a distance, were struck by this inescapable link between his life of prayer and the power of his ministry; and prayer for him, 'uttered or unexpressed', was this continual, daily, hourly recognition of his dependence upon the sovereignty of God.

2. The authority of Scripture.

In his attitude towards the Bible, Bash revealed a certain contradiction. On the one hand, his confidence in it as the Word of God was unshakeable. While it would be unfair to label him as a fundamentalist, because the rigid literalism which is associated with that title was absent in him, his love and reverence for the Bible were among the greatest and most formative influences of his life.

On the other hand he was not a great Bible student. There were, it must be admitted, fairly large tracts of Scripture which he never explored in any depth. He was like an explorer who, having discovered a new country, was content to live on the fertile coastal fringe. He knew that behind him in the hinter land were vast areas containing great treasures, but his excursions into them were spasmodic, and he regarded them as intended for other people at other times. Bash never for one moment doubted the veracity of, say, the Minor Prophets, or such books as Leviticus, Esther, Ecclesiastes and Revelation, or questioned their authority; but he did not spend very much time in them partly because he was enjoying himself so much elsewhere, and partly because they were of less value and significance to him in his principle life work which was to find scriptural answers to the problems and questions of sinful men and women. In this field, as in so many others, his approach was that of the pragmatist.

Of course, he always enjoyed tracing the loving purposes of God from the first days of man's disobedience to the coming of Christ, and could see 'the scarlet thread' running through Scripture from start to finish; but apart from the famous Old Testament stories like Noah and Abraham, the Passover and the Brazen Serpent, Rahab and Naaman, he was never very interested in the more detailed forms of typology. The importance of the Old Testament to him was the way it illustrated and foreshadowed the New: 'The New is in the Old concealed: the Old is in the New revealed'. It would I think be true to say that in his personal life he regarded the epistles as his workshop, the gospels (and especially St John) as his normal residence, and the psalms as his holiday retreat, where he loved to relax and to rejuvenate himself spiritually.

I must not trespass on an earlier chapter by discussing Bash as a speaker, but it should be said here that his talks were always noted for their scriptural basis and content. He never liked a talk to start without a verse from the Bible, and many of his best were those in which he would expound a passage verse by verse or phrase by phrase. Such was his belief in the power of the Bible, that he felt that if his own words were forgotten (which they seldom were) those of Scripture would find a permanent lodging in the hearts and minds of his hearers.

It was for this reason that he encouraged the learning of verses by heart, and the teaching of texts and the repeating of them parrot-fashion became an integral part of the daily Prayers he held at his camps. The practice, which sounds a very juvenile one to attempt amongst teenagers, was rescued from any embarrassment by his own inimitable way of doing it and by his inextinguishable sense of humour; and he always 'got away with it'.

His reverence for Scripture was immense. He deplored any sort of jokes about the Bible, and though he was quick to see the funny side of many incidents, and could make the stories live in a vivid, humorous and unforgettable way, anything approaching flippancy aroused his distaste and even his anger.

Many who heard him speak will remember the old, black, Authorised Version from which so many of his talks were given – some of its well-used pages already loose, and dotted about with pencilled comments. It was found among his other possessions after his death – a collector's piece for a spiritual museum. He knew so much of the King James version by heart, that it was difficult for him to come to terms with any of the newer translations, though J.B. Phillips greatly appealed to him for reference.

3. The divinity of Christ.

Once again this was a truth which in Bash's mind never admitted of argument, or upon which he entertained the smallest doubt. For him, as for the writer of Hebrews, Jesus Christ was 'the radiance of God's glory, and the exact representation of his being.' Now and then, it is true, that in his desire to simplify doctrine for the benefit of the young, the discerning could detect traces of Sabellianism, or some other confusion of the Persons of the Trinity; but in this branch of his faith, as in all others, he stood in the main-line tradition of protestant and anglican orthodoxy.

The extent to which the truth about the deity of Christ had taken root in his mind is well illustrated by his attitude towards the resurrection of the Lord. Many, perhaps most, Christians regard the resurrection as the crowning proof of Christ's divinity. It is what C.S. Lewis called 'The Grand Miracle', and if this can be accepted upon the evidence of Scripture, then so can all the other miracles, and with them the unique relationship of Jesus to his Father.

But this argument never appealed to Bash. He rarely preached about the resurrection, because his argument started at the other end. Because he already believed in the divinity of Christ, the resurrection had to take place, for 'it was not possible for death to retain him in its grip'. Most Christians find that the assurance of Christ's divinity flows from their belief in the resurrection, but for Bash it was the other way round, and he would say, 'I don't see why you make so much of it; it had to happen'.

The divinity of Christ had direct and important bearings upon his practical Christian living. It was while he was still in his teens that he received Christ as his personal Saviour, but it was only a few years later, while having tea in D.H. Evans in Oxford Street, that he fully acknowledged Christ as Master and Lord and, as he would put it, 'handed over to him the keys of every room in the house of his life'. It can only be said by those who knew him, that there was never a day when they were not reminded by the quality of his life, and his self-dedication to the cause of Christ, how real and deep that surrender must have been. The deity of Christ for Bash was not some dry theological concept, to be hammered out intellectually in lecture hall or study. It had immensely practical implications, and he more than most could echo those words of C.T. Studd, 'If Christ be God and died for me, then no sacrifice is too great for me to make for him.'

4. The centrality of the cross.

'If Christ be God and died for me . . .' Those words sum up what Bash believed about the cross. For him the atonement was the occasion when Jesus Christ accepted from his Father the judgement and punishment which a righteous God had to impose upon sinful man.

This is not to suggest that he failed to appreciate and to mention other aspects and dimensions of that first Good Friday. The death of Jesus in his view was a piece of matchless courage and unselfish love; and none who heard his famous talk on 'The seven words from the cross' will forget the moving way in which he pointed out that it was only after Jesus had thought of his enemies ('Father forgive them. . .'), his fellow-sufferer ('Today you shall be with me. . .') and his mother ('Son, behold your mother. . .') that he began to think of himself and to call for something to relieve his thirst.

Again, he saw the cross as the supreme demonstration of God's love, and he liked to preach on Romans 5.8 – 'God displays his love for us in this: while we were yet sinners, Christ died for us.' This never failed to move him, and he could not understand how people failed to be stirred emotionally as they surveyed the wondrous cross.

But Bash realised that the scriptural doctrine of the atonement is not merely subjective, but objective; for not only did it affect people's feelings, it altered facts about them. By dying on the cross, Jesus 'opened the kingdom of heaven to all believers'. The great cry of desolation ('My God, my God . . .') showed what our sins did to Jesus; while the cry of triumph that followed ('It is finished') demonstrated what Christ had done to our sins – put them away for ever, out of sight, out of reach and out of mind.

I wonder how many scores of times he must have illustrated this truth by reference to Isaiah 53.6. His right hand would be raised to represent himself, and his Bible (and I think this may have been why he always favoured a black one) would be placed upon it to represent our sins – the sins of the whole world. Pointing to this with his hand, he would quote the first part of the verse: 'All we like sheep have gone astray, we have turned every one to his own way'. Then the left hand would be raised to represent Jesus, in whom there was no sin, and, transferring the Bible from one hand to the other, he would finish the quotation, 'and the Lord has laid on him – that is on Jesus – the iniquity of us all.'

He first heard this illustration, so he used to say, from a visiting speaker at Cambridge, but he made it is own in a very special way, and those of us who have used it since, as I suppose most of his friends have, feel that the copyright still very much belongs to Bash.

But it sums up more completely than any words can do what he believed about the cross. The death of Jesus was absolutely central to his message. This was the gospel, the good news God has for mankind; and, as he loved to say, that is why we celebrate as Good Friday what would otherwise be 'Bad Friday'. The cross was 'the way back to God from the darkness of sin', or, as he sometimes put it, 'the only way to Mansion House is via King's Cross'.

But for Bash the cross was very much more than a starting-handle. It was the mainspring. It was not for him just the way in, but the way on; for throughout his ministry, with its ceaseless round of travelling, speaking, visiting and writing, it was the 'love of Christ that constrained him', and, as he used to tell us (airing his limited knowledge of Greek) the word for 'constrain' is the same as the word that is used to describe the crowd 'thronging' Jesus – almost sweeping him off his feet. For Bash the cross was central to his living as well as his teaching; it controlled the man as well as the message.

5. The necessity for the new birth.

One of Bash's foundational beliefs was this: 'Unless a man be born again, he cannot enter (he cannot even see) the kingdom of God.' This was the discovery that lit up the soul of Whitefield in the eighteenth century, and made him a tireless preacher of the new birth throughout Britain and America. This was the discovery that made Bash the most dedicated evangelist to public schoolboys that the twentieth century has known. He realized that they might be athletic, well bred, intellectual, able, religious, baptized and confirmed, and still be strangers to the kingdom of God. This is a very unacceptable doctrine in any civilised country. It made Bash highly suspect in some areas of the ecclesiastical and academic establishment, just as it drove Whitefield from the churches into the fields. The Englishman, and supremely the public schoolboy, amongst whom most of Bash's ministry was concentrated, is a Pelagian at heart. He believes instinctively that he is a good fellow, marred, maybe, by a few failings. Bash knew full well that 'the heart of man is deceitful above all things and desperately wicked', and that nothing short of a radical new birth could bring any of us into the presence of God; and this he taught fearlessly, quietly and thoughtfully and with tremendous effect throughout his ministry. He led hundreds of boys and young men into the experience of the new birth; and to bring people to this discovery, and to nourish them in the new relationship it introduced, were the twin passions of his life.

Although Bash was no great writer, he did produce two little books which embodied those twin passions. One was called 'How to succeed in the Christian life', and its title was aptly illustrated by its opening words: 'The Christian life is like riding a bicycle. If you don't go forward, you fall off'. The other booklet, 'Life at its Best' was designed to help people over the threshold into the new life. It had an enormous influence. It began precisely where the schoolboy found himself. It used the appropriate language. It dealt with the most pressing questions. And it made the way to a living faith inescapably clear, even to the point of suggesting a prayer of commitment, and the first steps forward from there. Not only did this booklet bring large numbers of people to Christ, but it lay behind a whole generation of evangelistic approaches that followed. Several of Bash's friends, including some contributors to this biography, have written evangelistic booklets which have been widely used; but all of them show the imprint of 'Life at its Best' and its influence. Bash was a past-master at clear, reasonable, unemotional but intensely challenging evangelism. He was gripped by the need for the new birth, and he had the utmost clarity in presenting the way to that new birth to all and sundry, but especially to the public schoolboy. It was 'the one thing needful' and in faithfulness to his Master, he could not do other than keep it in the forefront of his mind and of his teaching, however unpopular it proved to be in the chapels and common rooms of the public schools. If Jesus had said 'You must be born again', then clearly you *must*.

6. The responsibility of man.

In the classical tradition of all great evangelists, Bash prayed as though everything depended upon God and preached as though it all depended upon man. For him this presented no contradiction. Like Charles Simeon, he saw no *via media* between predestination and free will, but was content to believe them both equally, looking upon them as two sides of an arch which were joined in heaven, or two parallel lines meeting in infinity.

The strength and depth of his own convictions made it hard for him to understand and appreciate the person with genuine intellectual difficulties – the honest doubter. He did not find it easy to put himself in such a person's place, and was apt to regard all intellectual problems as a kind of smokescreen behind which a man could retreat from the challenge of Christ, while all the time the real reason for such evasive action was pride, perhaps, or the fear of man, or some secretly cherished sin.

It must be admitted that as often as not he was right, and many who tried to escape under cover of intellectual doubts came later to confess that this was not the real reason. But as time went on, I think he became more sympathetic to the genuine 'Thomas', and would humbly encourage someone who he felt was better equipped than he was himself to talk with the person concerned and try to help him out of the mists of agnosticism.

His study of Scripture had convinced him that in man's own hands had been placed the power to choose his own destiny – an eternity with Christ or without him. Conversion, or the new birth, was not an optional extra, but a basic necessity. Concerning those who had never had the chance to hear of Christ, or the mental capacity to understand, his stance was as reserved as Scripture; but to those who were given that chance to hear and the ability to understand, the awesome truth was burned upon his heart, 'How shall we escape if we neglect so great a salvation.'

* * * * *

These six things therefore were the foundation of Bash's theology. They were the rock on which his whole life and philosophy were built – the things he most surely believed, and of which he spoke throughout his long ministry with the utmost conviction and sincerity.

He gave very little time and space in his thinking to what might be called 'speculative theology' which for some Christians can have an inordinate attraction, but which he regarded as unhelpful and disputatious. We have already seen that typology only made a limited appeal to him, and the same was true of eschatology. He rarely ventured an opinion, and then only tentatively, about the shape of 'the last things'. For him heaven was to be with Christ and hell to be without him, and that was really all he seemed anxious to know. Speculation about the Second Coming, and arguments about prophecy and about pre- or post-millenialism he was content to leave to others.

And he refused to be side-tracked. What are sometimes called 'the social implications of the gospel' did not, he felt concern him, beyond a desire to be a law-abiding citizen and a kind-hearted neighbour. He dared not let such matters distract him from his supreme calling to be an evangelist and a pastor; and in any case in his view the only way to get better measures, economic and political, was to get better men.

In the same way, he was apt to regard with suspicion and even mistrust what many felt to be new and important insights and emphases. For example, he entertained grave misgivings about the so-called 'Charismatic Movement' which some of his friends thought he had not perhaps studied in sufficient depth.

If we turn to moral theology, we can see again the influence of Scripture, for it was based firmly on the Ten Commandments, amplified and emphasised by the teaching of the New Testament. There was a distinctly puritanical (though never censorious) streak about him. In common perhaps with most Christians, but long before it was recognised as a hazard to health, he had dismissed smoking as a dangerous habit. He would never touch alcohol, while cards, the theatre and even novels were recreations he never sought for himself, though it is fair to say that as time went on he evinced an increasing tolerance and sympathy towards those who thought differently from himself on these matters. Some of them he might even have enjoyed, had it not been for that ever-present fear which he could not escape of putting a stumbling-block in the way of a younger and more fragile Christian.

He held very strong views about Sunday. He always liked to be seen in a suit on that day – light enough to dispel any idea that he was going to a funeral, but not so light that it suggested he was off to the races; while games, newspapers and travelling (except in the exercise of his ministry) were things he always tried to avoid. Not all his friends and followers went along with him over this, but few can have resented the firm and yet gentle way in which his convictions were held, and probably most felt in their hearts that he was making a worth while stand against the long, slow, drawling tides of drift and surrender which were undermining traditional standards and values.

In matters ecclesiastical, his home was the Church of England. He loved it for its doctrine, for its faithfulness to Scripture, its traditions and its dignity; but here, as in so much else, he was a pragmatist, and apart from all these things, he regarded it as the best boat to fish from. He was not therefore in any sense of the word a bigoted churchman. For most of his life he worked very happily in a society which was interdenominational, and some of his greatest spiritual heroes were members of churches other than his own.

Nor was there anything of the 'Hot Prot' about him. While eschewing much of the doctrine of Roman Catholicism, he preferred to dwell upon the things in that church of which he approved. 'I've been thinking of all the things I like about Roman Catholics', he was heard to say once. And he made light of some of the things which fussed and bothered more sensitive evangelicals. It did not worry him in the least, if it was the custom of the church to do so, to turn east to say the Creed, and to bow at the name of Jesus.

But 'attending church' was perhaps not his strongest point. On the rare occasions when he was free to do so, he seldom attended a church service unless he knew in advance that the preacher would appeal to him; and even then he had the disconcerting habit of arriving just in time for the sermon, and as likely as not slipping out again before the collection; and he would greatly have appreciated the remark that was made at his funeral, that it was a change to see him in time for a service. 'Worship', in the narrow and limited sense in which we apply that word to church attendance did not mean a very great deal to him; but in the wider sense of recognizing the lordship of Christ in every department of daily life, it meant everything in the world.

The same was to some extent true of his attitude towards the sacraments. He was a firm believer in Infant Baptism, and he must have helped many young men to understand the covenant theology on which it is based. He saw the service as essentially scriptural (particularly in the light of infant circumcision in the Old Testament), but to be taken as only one side of a covenant or treaty, the other being Confirmation.

It was difficult to discern in his thoughts about Holy Communion any theology much beyond that of Zwingli. The service for him was essentially one of remembrance and thanksgiving, and he felt that too much emphasis upon it detracted from its value, and turned it into a pair of spiritual crutches on which people came to rely too much, instead of developing that close, inner and continual walk with the Lord which was so characteristic of him. 'It's not chapel, man, it's abiding', he is reported to have replied to a friend who tried to rouse him early one morning from beneath the bed-clothes in order to attend a service at Ridley Hall.

On the occasions when he himself was the celebrant, none could fail to be impressed with the beautiful and dignified way in which he conducted the service, almost every word and phrase weighted with meaning and measured, almost as though he were doing it for the first time; which was not quite true. It contrasted favourably with those whose celebration of this lovely sacrament has grown almost too familiar and mechanical, perhaps because they have done it too often.

It would be impossible to end this chapter without some reference to the man who, more than any other, had such a powerful influence upon Bash during his spiritually formative years. R.A. Torrey was a friend and disciple of the great American evangelist, D.L. Moody. In many ways they complemented each other, and those who knew them both would probably say that Moody conveyed warmth and Torrey light.

Unlike Moody, Torrey was a highly cultured and educated man, who had studied long and deeply, and whose writings have probably given him a greater permanent influence than his more famous predecessor; and there is no doubt at all about the debt Bash owed to him, and admitted that he owed.

A deeply spiritual man, Torrey had the gift of speaking and writing with the utmost clarity and simplicity. As an ex-lawyer, his logic was devastating, and his style direct, uncomplicated and lucid. There were other writers like S.D. Gordon and F.B. Meyer from whom Bash obviously benefitted, but it was always the great Dr Torrey who held first place in his esteem, and to whom he would turn again and again; and those of us who owe so much to Bash should also acknowledge our debt to his own spiritual mentor.

There was little that Torrey wrote which Bash did not devour and disseminate, with one exception. Later on in his ministry Torrey came into a deeper experience of the Holy Spirit, which he called 'Baptism with the Spirit', and which was associated with speaking in tongues. In many ways his preaching on holiness was a precursor of the Pentecostal movement that was soon to break out in Azusa Street, Los Angeles. This emphasis on 'tongues', and a second stage movement of the Holy Spirit seemed instinctively wrong to Bash. 'Poor Torrey went loopy', he would say with a smile. But with that sole exception, the influence of Torrey was strong in much of his own thinking and speaking.

It is absurd to think of either Torrey or Bash as theologians in any sense other than the very broad one with which we started this chapter. Both were almost entirely innocent of any technical theology; and yet both possessed what so many professional theologians lack – balance, and what Bash himself would have called 'a sense of smell'. He had an almost instinctive hunch about the significant truths of the Christian faith, and the ability to communicate them simply and effectively to others.

Time and again in my own theological studies I have come back to a position advanced to me years before at Bash's knee. It was he who taught me not to talk about 'conversions' (which no man can be sure of in others), but 'professions of conversion'. He taught me to distinguish between the human elements in conversion (repentance and faith) and the divine side (the gift of God's Spirit in regeneration). He taught me to see that salvation has three tenses, and that it is incorrect for anyone to say 'I am saved' *tout simple.* 'I have been saved from the guilt of sin by Christ's death upon the cross', he would say, 'I am being saved from the power of sin by his Spirit within me, and one day I shall be saved from the very presence of sin when I go to be with him in heaven.'

Well, he who taught this with such unresearched acumen now enjoys the third tense of salvation, and he has left behind him a generation of men in various areas of Christian ministry and leadership who thank God for this man who has such a powerful influence for God. Like the beloved apostle Paul, Bash's own faults were obvious, and in many ways engaging. Yet his greatness lay in his recognition of his own weakness and his total dedication to the Christ whom he sought to know and love more and more. That single-minded dedication to his Lord, which I saw so clearly in Bash, has been the greatest single influence on my own life. Hundreds perhaps thousands could say the same; and perhaps that is the supreme goal of theology: so to know about God that you know him, and so to know him that you reflect him.

9: A woman's view

Mary Mullins

David and Mary Mullins were married in South Africa, and returned home to live in Oxford and now in Lymington. David was one of Bash's most trusted medical advisers, while Mary for many years helped with the domestic work at Iwerne Minster. In the 1960's she started and became responsible for the girls' camps which until recently were held at Motcombe Park, not far from Iwerne Minster, and now take place each summer at Marsh Court, Stockbridge.

9: A woman's view

We were to arrive in time for tea. It was my first visit as a young wife, to Iwerne. 'What will it be like?' I wondered, and as we turned into the drive, a mixture of apprehension and excitement arose. There was the house, both rather grand and ugly as a first impression, and typically Victorian. 'What', I kept wondering to myself, 'will Bash be like?' My father's stories of their years together at Ridley Hall in the early twenty's presented a rather eccentric figure. I was eager to meet this man whose influence upon my husband was so great, and whose work amongst school boys was obviously both strategic and important. After all, hadn't David said it would be our priority Christian work before he proposed to me? Bash was to be a major influence upon my own life and work, and I was still a little uncertain of this influence.

The library was full of people, mostly under thirty, and predominantly school boys. There he was, unmistakeably, talking to one of the boys on the other side of the room. The only person over fifty; tall, slim, quiet and softly spoken, with grey hair going bald, and with a humourous twinkle in his brown eyes. He was chatting away with animation and ease. Then our moment had come. It was our first meeting face to face. It was very important to David, who had only been able to consult Bash about our marriage by telegram from South Africa. It was not easy for Bash, faced with someone's bride of nearly a year, and knowing David would want his approval. 'What will he think?' I wondered, 'What will he say?'. In fact, he said very little, and the memory of what he said has faded into the mists of the past. I only remember that all the other women who had come as helpers were having tea elsewhere, and my presence was rather an embarrassment to him. David was asked to shew me where I should be. A brief but historic encounter. As I moved away, I wondered how he would come over to the boys.

In his earlier years, Bash often spoke of women in a decidedly derogatory manner. They were not the people he usually chose to take into his confidence. He assumed they were not interested in the details which concerned their men, though he appreciated any backing up given, especially if it meant the right sort of food, for meals at Iwerne, or teas in term-time; but he gave the impression that he thought women were second class citizens.

In his childhood Bash had little or no friendly contacts with girls of his own age. As a young man he was accustomed to being surrounded by the maids, his mother – a capable woman with leadership qualities which she exercised in the church as the vicar's wife, apparently speaking at meetings with power, – and his aunt, known as 'Pussy', who never married, and who lived all her life with Bash and his mother. None of his other near relations married. This may well be part of the reason why, generally speaking, he preferred a man's company. He clearly felt smothered, even dominated by his mother, though he gave warm commendation to 'Pussy': 'she prayed for me every day', and she played with him and his brothers when they were children. He was clearly spoilt. During her lifetime, one sensed that old Mrs. Nash was rather a bother and a nuisance. Did Bash only realise when she died just how devoted he was to her, and how deeply he missed her? Certainly her death caused him quite a long period of serious depression.

During the early stages of his life-work, we now know that there was a time when marriage was seriously contemplated (only the woman of his choice apparently never knew it.) The devotion Bash shewed to God and his calling to this work, is demonstrated well by the fact that he chose to forfeit marriage for the Kingdom of Heaven's sake.

There were other women less well known to most people to whom we all owe a great deal, for they cared for him throughout his life-time after his mother's death. Mrs. Drake was perhaps the woman whose years of devotion exceeded all others. She had long been helping at 10 Crauford Rise before Mrs. Nash died. Afterwards she moved in, and lived and worked there as his housekeeper until she herself had to retire, and died only a short time before he did.

Mary McIver was the person who nursed and cared for him most recently. Hers was a dedicated service of loyalty and devotion to the end of his life. In his confusion, he sometimes thought she was a man, but right up to the end, in his clearer moments, his impish humour would bubble up. Not long before he died, Mary decided it was time to remind him that there might not be many more days for him on earth. He said nothing at the time, but later in the day when Mary went to see how he was, he looked up, and with a mischievious sparkle in his eyes he said 'Not yet Mary, not yet!'

These women were very devoted to Bash. Both clearly saw his greatness, and were glad to be of service to God through their care and hard work for him. It is worth a moment's thought how great our debt to them actually was, for theirs was the 'hidden humble job in the background, without which his ministry might have been less effective.

Knowing something of this limited social contact with women, it is easier to understand the awkwardness he felt with them, and which perhaps lay behind his behaviour toward them. Most women sensed he would prefer not to have to greet them if he could courteously avoid doing so, and that he had more important things on his mind than small talk with a woman. It must in fairness be stressed that this was the impression he made on *younger* women; with his contemporaries and with those who were older, he was always perfectly relaxed and at ease, and from one of them he was even obliged to decline an offer of marriage.

But to return to that first camp I attended in 1953. For most women, the work at Iwerne was in one sense very well known. They saw how spiritually mature these men were; how seriously they took the demands Christ made on them; they noticed the powerful effects of the workings of the Holy Spirit in the lives of the men they encountered, as well as the competence and quiet confidence most of them displayed, both in their knowledge of the truth and in their clear cut presentation of it. All these things were clearly visible to any woman who had eyes to see and ears to hear, and they were generally profoundly impressed. In this sense then, the work was well known to those outside, myself included. The unknown was the method Bash used to teach; to instil such dedication to the vision of God's work; and particularly to inspire the loyalty and devotion of the team who worked with him. This frequently led to curiosity and a sense of wonderment. For most women, the chance to find out the answers for themselves was rare if not impossible, as the role of women at Iwerne was confined to a dozen or so who helped domestically at each camp.

Regrettably, and perhaps inevitably, this led to sporadic outbreaks of stories circulating about Bash which were often only hearsay. In turn these became gossip, which had either distorted or exaggerated the truth, or, occasionally, it would be discovered that some tale had been entirely fabricated. Having heard and believed many of these accounts myself when I was a girl, I was to learn that they were the result of misguided and sadly sometimes, unkindly intentions arising from ignorance and perhaps through people being envious of the effective work amongst men and boys, which seemed to be too exclusive. I use the word 'seemed' advisedly, because this was an impression gained from outside the work. It was a superficial judgement. It was inaccurate to offer as a criticism, based as it was upon little knowledge either of Bash or his work. Elsewhere in this book no doubt, something about Bash's unashamed exclusiveness will have been enlarged upon.

One of the most recurring themes over the years has been that Bash was a woman-hater. This is an example of the harm gossip does, as it was simply not true. Certainly Bash was shy with most girls, and for many it appeared as if he was not as concerned for them as he was for their brothers, which was sad. Now I found myself on the inside, and knew I would be able to see for myself, I hoped, what Bash was really like. I was young and prejudiced, so my impressions were somewhat biased. I felt rather flat, especially when I was ushered into a large, cold dormitory at the top of the house to be shared with five other girls. Camp had begun.

It ought to be explained that in the early days of his camps Bash used to employ local domestic help to cope with the cleaning and cooking. It was only after the war that the wives, fiancées and sisters of officers began to emerge as voluntary helpers. Our ambiguous and unsatisfactory position was therefore to some extent due to the fact that we came during a transition period, when no clear policy had been reached regarding the role of the lady-helpers. Before he retired, a very different pattern had been established.

The greatest help was that there were three of us who were brides at that camp, on our first visit. Hilary Knight and Jane Tupper shared in the frustrations, jokes and revelations which were to follow.

Much of that first camp is remembered with clarity. It was an education for us three to learn more intimately, how the work was run; to see for ourselves the impeccable efficiency of every part of the work, and the importance attached to the smallest detail even, on the practical side. I learnt in greater depth, the value of doing some humble, often unseen task, to the glory of God. I was deeply impressed.

It was also a difficult time, especially being discouraged from joining our husbands when our work was done. This was hard as well as strange, as we were entirely convinced, before we went to Iwerne of the value of the work. We wanted to see more of its outworking first hand. This was frustrating, for there was a weakness here.

Bash's wisdom and shrewdness in his advice about marriage would not be disputed in general terms, for he helped many to see their calling in the service of God as a priority. The execution of his principles and his behaviour however, have left their mark and to a surprising degree, still do, in a not altogether helpful way upon many young men. Instead of taking his advice sensibly, many have taken it to extremes.

'The girls are here to work, and so are you' he would rightly say to a team at the start of a camp; but he expected his younger men to limit their conversation with the girls to a polite greeting if they passed them. He personally never spoke to us unless he had to. He was clearly embarrassed by our presence and preferred to avoid us if he could. It would be true to say, that if not in word, certainly by his example, his influence upon some people in this area has been harmful. So careful have they been not to become over involved with girls too soon, that many have failed to become involved enough, and have found themselves both awkward and embarrassed in the company of girls in their mid-twenties or even older. This has not helped the gossip, but rather has provided some justifiable criticism to the detriment of Bash and some of his men. He failed to see the need to provide opportunities for his team to meet and work with girls in the natural way necessary to young people, and this legacy has remained.

But it must not be assumed from this that Bash's attitude towards marriage was negative and unhelpful. It is true he counselled caution, and preferred men to marry in their late rather than their early twenties, but all who came to him for advice would testify to the sympathy and wisdom which he showed, encouraging them to go forward, or perhaps preventing them from making a mistake. The remarkable success of what might be called 'camp marriages' is an eloquent witness to the standard of his guidance in this matter.

After that first camp, I was asked if I could help at the next one also 'just this once' as helpers were short. I eventually helped at every camp for the next five years. I learnt an increasing amount. Some changes were made to the domestic scene, the most important and beneficial being the inclusion of the helpers at prayers in the mornings as well as in the evenings. Attending every prayers, rather than only the evening ones, enabled us to learn more and pray more intelligently. It also made us a little more involved. We were also allowed to attend the Bible Readings when free. Philip Thompson was the greatest help in these two things and I recall many conversations in the office, discussing ways and means of improving things for the women.

I learnt countless tasks, from managing the team of helpers to washing up and cleaning baths. During those years, I had a unique and unsought training in every practical aspect of the work, even doing the cooking for the advance party at the start of camp. As a result, I was able to learn more of the many sides to Bash. He used to slip into the kitchen, hoping, one had the feeling, that no one, except perhaps the quartermaster, would be there. As often as not he wasn't there, so one of us would be approached: 'Mary, do you think there would be one slim slice of bacon I might have?' and then offering from behind his back, somewhat sheepishly, a plate upon which he hoped it would be placed. Then, when the bacon was discovered; 'do you think you could possibly spare *two* slices?'

Other sides to him too I discovered. One time at the start of a camp before any of the boys had arrived, 'Mary, do you think you could find some flowers to put in —'s room? He works so hard for us all here, and I know he likes flowers. . .' I was struck by his care of individuals and attention to details concerning them and the courteous approaches he made to me, mindful of the other tasks I had to do.

Again, thinking only for the best for one man in his team whose fiancée he knew I knew too: 'Mary, she wears lipstick I noticed. Do you think she's *really* 'keen'? Will she make a good, supportive wife for him?'

To have had a nursing training provided an entré to Bash which gave a rare opportunity to a woman to know him better still. Part of the nurses' role at Iwerne was to do certain small personal tasks for him. These were not very many, but it soon became apparent that his cool reserve was removed when he knew you were the nurse. At least, that has been the guess made as to why, as nurses, some of us found him more relaxed than others did.

Besides the entertainment of discussing the relative merits of one brand of bed-time drink with another, (it was amusing to suggest a new one each camp if possible, and see if he could be persuaded to change from his most recent preference) there were the various medical needs which were sometimes discussed. Being the wife of one of his favourite doctors produced a number of ridiculous and very funny situations. There was the telephone call one afternoon at home when Bash needed medical advice. 'Mary, could you ask David if I might safely use the cough mixture he gave me for a cough which went like . . .' pause, then in a completely different tone '. . . "oohuh, oohuh"' . . . then, following another pause he continued . . . 'for a cough which now goes "ihhih, ihhih"'?

Aside from these diversions there was the opportunity at Iwerne to observe at close quarters some of the things which most women only ever heard second-hand from their husbands or brothers; his tidiness; his orderly arrangement of lists, books, papers and other camp necessities around his room. It always reminded me of Churchill's 'operation room' at Chartwell. There was a battle on, and we must be ready for anything.

After about three years of limited encounters with Bash (I have to admit it took all those years) I began to appreciate his spiritual power which I had observed before, but only now began to realise the full extent of its greatness.

His were the talks which penetrated my own heart more than any others. His winsomeness, and ability to get inside the minds of his hearers, as well as his simple yet penetrating and potent descriptive powers, were some of the things which humbled, convicted and taught me.

It was around this time that I had the privilege of being invited into his room to discuss the possible start of a similar camp for girls. It came as a complete surprise. I was delighted and excited. Here I learnt for the first time, and was privileged to share in, the full measure of his vision and devotion. He gave me unlimited time in order to impart these to me. He was wise and understanding. He was patient and endlessly helpful to me. At such an important moment his counsel was of incalculable value to the girls work soon to be launched. He would write out lists of talks; suggest Bible Readings; draw up papers to explain the truths behind the subjects, as well as the importance of the content of each talk.

During these months of preparation for me, and once it was established that the girls camp would take place, Bash was willing to create seemingly endless precedents so that I might learn from Iwerne. He invited Margaret Butterworth and Margaret Saunders (née Talbot-Rice) who were to be the Leader and Secretary respectively, to come to Iwerne. Together we were able to observe and ask questions about anything. We were invited into all the Bible Readings, Officers' Meetings and Prayer meetings. Even though it is now over twenty years since I took on the leadership of our own meetings, I cannot emulate his style, nor have I yet perfected the methods he used. The only thing I never witnessed was a Dormitory Time of Quiet (though I did once eavesdrop outside a room).

There seemed to be no end to the lessons I could learn. Bash recommended Chaplains; he warned, he encouraged. He predicted with remarkable insight and accuracy that it would take ten years to establish the work, and another ten before we would be working within the schools we aimed to reach. He even came to speak to our first team of leaders on 'How to give a Talk'. This was in some ways an ordeal for him – talking to a room full of girls – but he carried it off with his customary good humour and naturalness. The talk was memorable and thankfully, recorded for posterity.

Bash was positively comic when introduced to small children. I vividly recall his first encounter with our first baby. After a polite pause to take a look inside the pram, he crooked his forefinger and bent over the pram. 'Cuckoo' he called, and followed it by a polite generality such as 'Isn't she sweet?' which as his considered opinion was altogether unconvincing. It seemed funny enough for our first child. By the time he met our fourth baby, we were able to predict with confidence to the elder three, what he would say and do. He did not disappoint them. Nor, we discovered from other families, did his greeting vary with countless other babies. He showed genuine interest in our family's progress and education. As they grew older we valued his wise, shrewd and mostly timely advice. The one notable exception being when he discovered our elder son had Down's Syndrome. Here, with hindsight it seems he was out of his depth. He recommended in the strongest terms that he should be placed without further delay, in a home. He never knew how much pain that piece of advice caused. He had clearly thought he was being helpful, and had genuinely fancied this might be a good idea. What he had failed to consider was that we regarded this baby, not as a mistake, but, just as much as our first child, as God's good gift to us and a special privilege. He seemed not to realise our instinctive love for him and desire at least to try to care for him at home.

It is good to be able to record that on what turned out to be our last visit to him a few months before he died, he went out of his way to include this son of ours. We had been to watch a demonstration of the Riding for the Disabled of which our son had been a part, showing a number of different skills, at a nearby centre. Bash took an obvious interest in what he had been doing, and talked to him with real vivacity. Before we left, he gave him a present. It was a momento Bash had brought home from his first ever Swiss party skiing with his boys. He treated him with the same kindness and grace as he treated us, as his equal.

This was one of his great strengths. Whenever his advice was rejected, he never referred to it again, and accepted the decision made with no further comment, except of a positive nature.

A strong protagonist for the independent schools, he encouraged us in our decisions for our childrens' education, in part at least for the value, as he saw it, of the Christian link this brought to the school.

His visits to our home were regular when we lived in Oxford, usually once or twice a term. These were chiefly to attend tea parties or coffee parties provided for thirty or forty undergraduates. He would arrive, usually rather late, and move straight into the scene. Bash's eccentricities over food led to some amusingly outrageous behaviour. He once telephoned to ask if he could lunch with us. The meal was already on the table. I readily agreed, though perhaps unwisely added that we were having a simple lunch of soup and cheese. He arrived shortly afterwards. When he had politely consumed a bowl of soup, he slipped his hand into his jacket pocket saying as he withdrew a large paper packet 'Mary, I have brought with me, some rather nice ham, – would you like some?' and he passed the packet to me. It was noteworthy, not only for providing his own preferred lunch and producing it in the middle of a meal, but also for his thoughtful generosity as he had accurately catered for all the hungry family, who were of course, delighted.

In no way could Bash be described as 'a ladies' man.' Quite the reverse. It is in many ways all the more to his credit, or perhaps more correctly, to the glory of God, that despite his lack of ease with women, and his eccentricities, he nevertheless earned the respect and affection of so many of us. He was not a man one would turn to look at for a second time – unless he had been pointed out as one of the most outstanding men in the Christian world.

10: The ambassador for Christ

John Pollock

At the end of the War, John Pollock returned to Cambridge to prepare for Ordination, but before proceeding to take Holy Orders he took up a teaching post at Wellington. He then went as curate to St Paul's, Portman Square, but in due course left regular parish life to devote himself to writing. He is the author of many books, amongst the best known being *Moody without Sankey*, *Billy Graham*, and *The Good Seed*, which is a history of Scripture Union.

10: The ambassador for Christ

On Sunday 25th February 1940, in the cold winter of the 'phoney war' before the guns began in earnest, Bash drove up in his black Rover to a private house on the hill above Godalming, ready to speak to the Charterhouse Christian Union. In age he was rising forty-two. As he went down the stairs to the basement room, where the meeting was to take place, I and two other boys of my house, Derek and Hugh, were coming in. It would be my first attendance, apart from a couple of Sundays two years earlier, and I came with great anticipation because I had become a commited Christian in my best friend Derek's study, ten days earlier. Derek had made the same decision a week before that, and at once had shared his experience with me.

I was sixteen years old and in my third year at school. I came from a typical family of the time: a close-knit and very happy home where I and my two older brothers and a sister had been brought up to read the Bible and say our prayers. The Christian ethic was the backbone of my parents' life, even though they never talked about religion without embarrassment.

Bash was skilful at reaching boys from such homes; but it was before I met him, and through the indirect influence of the Christian Union, that I had accepted Christ after a long and painful struggle with religious pride and self-effort. When I followed Bash down the basement stairs I had already begun to discover the wonder of knowing the Lord Jesus as a Friend, and was hungering to know him better.

Bash took as his theme the Works of the Flesh and the Fruit of the Spirit, and he worked it out unemotionally in the context of a schoolboy's life. I was not in an observant mood to notice the carefully chosen Sunday suit, the quiet tie ('a loud tie interferes with the message') or his neatly brushed hair, but I had never heard Christian truth put so plainly and simply, with a quiet authority and no word wasted.

I had begun to write up a daily journal or diary at the start of 1940, not knowing what momentous events, personal and national, lay ahead. That night I wrote: 'Mr Nash (commonly known as Bash) spoke of how we must open every "room" in our minds to the Lord Jesus; and when I reflected I found that I had not done so. There were still one or two rooms where He was not. I had a short chat with Bash afterwards and Derek stayed on and spoke for an hour with him.' Derek had great potential as a leader but was killed in the closing days of the War.

Back in my house I attended the Sunday evening Bible Reading which we had begun while struggling towards faith, in the house tutor's room; 'and it was then,' I wrote in my diary, 'and not until then, I know, that I opened every door to the Lord Jesus. Then there descended on me such a quiet certainty, joy and peace of mind that I have never had before. Ten days ago I opened the "Front Door". Now every door is open, I feel sure.' Hugh, my other close friend, dates his conversion from Bash's talk that day: he survived the War and is a leading lawyer in commerce and an active Christian.

Nearly three weeks later Bash invited Derek, Hugh and myself to tea in Godalming, a few days before Hugh and I were to be confirmed in the chapel of Farnham Castle. I hurried down after a rehearsal for the school play. Bash had come by train, on a gusty day which threatened rain. 'We had a very cheerful meal and afterwards a BR. He so obviously is filled with the Holy Ghost and I am much strengthened whenever I meet him.' Afterwards I walked with him alone to the station and he urged me not to 'hot gospel', having discovered that I was sold on C. T. Studd (the house tutor, a cricketer, had lent me the biography) and rather too bubbling with the new wine.

I did not see Bash again until we all arrived at Camp, the first to be held at Iwerne Minster, on 9th April 1940, the day Denmark fell and Norway began her bitter but doomed resistance to Hitler. We reached the house at about 5 pm, to be welcomed by Bash in his blue shorts and Trinity field club blazer, with that blend of friendliness and authority which was specially his. I recorded: 'Everybody seems awfully nice, and it is easy to get to know people as everyone is out to get to know everyone else.' Hockey and ragger were great fun; a proof indeed of my conversion, for a few months earlier I would have loathed the thought of spending part of the holidays playing organized or disorganized games with other schoolboys. At prayers in the evening Bash spoke on the Parable of the Treasure hidden in the field. Once again each word counted and he never raised his voice.

I was in the dormitory of Douglas Argyle and Richard Rhodes-James. Every day I made new friends while far away the naval battles raged off Norway. On the Thursday John Earp gave a talk I have never forgotten. He spoke of the immensity of the universe until we felt utterly small; he spoke of the incredible detail of the tiniest molecule, and applied the analogy until I, for one, realized as never before the enormity of the slightest sin in the sight of God. It was a masterly exposition which led me to a true conviction of sin.

Bash followed on the next night with a 'wonderful talk on "Behold, I stand at the door and knock,"' the text from Revelation well known to generations of campers but always fresh in Bash's hands, as it was to me that night. And he spoke with such clarity and authority that I nearly tried to begin the Christian life all over again; I had been enjoying myself so much at Camp that the consciousness of Christ's presence had dimmed; I was still too young in the faith to discriminate between feelings and fact. Mercifully I pulled up in time. 'I nearly "ruined" myself later,' I recorded, 'by trying to relive my experience of February 15th, and by wondering whether I had taken the step after all. That was very foolish. One has only to look at the results experienced since that date.' This confusion did not re-occur when Bash taught me to pray in my heart for him and others as he spoke.

On the Sunday I attended the shortened early Service of Holy Communion which Bash conducted, with a large congregation, in the Clayesmore school chapel at Iwerne. I do not need my diary to recall the impact of his reading of the liturgy. At home and school the clerics of the day hurried at various speeds of gabble. Bash did not drag, but every syllable was clear; he prayed each of those lovely, centuries-old prayers with the same sincerity as he prayed extempore. I had never heard a parson use the alternative prayer for the Sovereign, but Bash was unforgettable as he prayed at that time of crisis: 'We humbly beseech thee so to dispose and govern the heart of George thy servant, our King and Governor, that in all his thoughts, words and works, he may ever seek thy honour and glory. . .'

At the morning service in the library, for the whole camp, I heard for the first time Bash's famous four point address on Moses: his call, his preparation, his work, and his sad fade out – 'a wonderful sermon, so helpful.'

My first Camp was over all too soon, and if Bash was inevitably a slightly remote figure to a new camper, I knew he was someone to trust, who could open fresh vistas whenever the opportunity came to meet him. I was therefore thrilled, back at Charterhouse, to receive a short note in his clear script in reply to my bread-and-butter letter. Bash wrote: 'I am so bucked that you found Camp such an inspiration. I *knew* you would enjoy it. As you say the grand atmosphere of freedom and peace when so many gather who know HIM is a revelation. And now you are back at school and I do hope it's going to be the happiest term you've ever had – happy because you're living each day with a new purpose – to please and serve HIM.' I had told him of my desire to be ordained after Cambridge (having abandoned my long standing ambition to follow the family and aim for the top of the legal tree) and he urged me not to read divinity but a subject like history, 'which is much more helpful in broadening one's mind.' Bash wisely did not attempt to explain that the divinity faculties of that era were destructively liberal.

The day after I had received Bash's letter the Germans invaded the Low Countries, Churchill became Prime Minister and the news looked darker each day, except for Churchill's indomitable leadership. I was able to bring an Austrian boy in my house to Christ; his world had collapsed at the Anschluss of 1938 and he had grown blacker in mind and looks as each German victory made the invasion of England more probable. The change when Otto trusted Christ was noticeable and I proudly presented him when Bash came to the Christian Union, now meeting in a pleasant Georgian drawing room, on 25th May. They talked together. Then Bash spoke to us on the soldier of the Lord Jesus and his armour, a highly appropriate theme for the weekend before Dunkirk.

The next day I went down with a bad attack of measles, and spent Britain's 'Finest Hour' ignominiously in the sanatorium, emerging on the day Paris fell. By then, Charterhouse was in the grip of invasion fever, digging a tank trap (in a marsh) and practising defence and fitting out air raid shelters and watching an aerial dog fight above our heads. We were all very determined, and had as unshakeable a faith in ultimate victory as Churchill, but in recording my decision to go to the school farming camp and then to Iwerne, which would also be a farming camp, I added: 'But of course, the Lord Jesus may work it out differently. After all, Hitler says he will be in London on 15th August, and every date he has given so far has been proved correct. But we are safe in the Lord Jesus.'

In the midst of all this I received a letter from Bash inviting me to meet him the next day. I wired acceptance.

We met in Godalming and drove to a secluded spot for the first unhurried chat I had ever had with him. He let me rush on about all we were doing, and then deflected my wilder ideas by a few pithy words of advice. And, I recorded, 'He told me how, when he wakes up every morning, he commits himself to the Lord Jesus asking that He will guide him to the right people through the day. A word here, a smile there, and opportunities taken all through the day, do much in the Great Campaign with and for Jesus.' He advised me to carry a copy of *Life at its Best,* just in case a chance came.

Altogether 'it was a grand time, and only disturbed for a few minutes by the noise of the German air raid on Aldershot and Thursley.' Derek and Hugh joined us for tea. Bash always picked a good place and knew how to encourage schoolboys to tuck in to sausages and cakes. Then we drove back to the secluded spot, except for Hugh who was due for guard duty, and 'had a cracking good QT together. We took 2 Corinthians 6.1-10, the Workers' Chapter. Bash teaches one so much. I had not looked at that chapter much before.'

During our earlier chat I had unknowingly come up against one of Bash's weaknesses. We were discussing my school work (I was in the History VIth) and he left me with the impression that the main point was to put my energy into our Christian efforts, and to glorify Christ simply by getting good marks. However, I happened to be a keen historian in a rather indifferent form with a charming but easygoing master, and Bash would have been wiser to have stressed the need to stretch my mind to work hard, and to see academic excellence as a vital step, in my case, to more fruitful service when grown up. I was naturally too inexperienced to realize that Bash was very much a man of his age, when evangelicals were scared of the intellect because liberalism rode high. It took me years to get my educational priorities right.

Meanwhile, despite that 'cracking good QT' my great friend and leader Derek was showing signs of backsliding, probably caused mainly by physical fatigue in that gruelling summer of the Battle of Britain. At first I could not fathom his moods and his arguing. Then on 17th July I had another letter from Bash. He encouraged me to expect great opportunities for Christian service and warned that Christ had many things to teach, and would 'humble me and draw me away from trust in myself. He may lead me through deep waters...' In my reply I asked what to do about Derek's backslide.

Four days later Bash spoke at the C.U., 'an excellent talk on our life being a Powerful thing, a Passing thing, and a Paid-for (or Redeemed) thing. It really was a grand talk and I hope has led some people to the Lord Jesus.' Afterwards we had a long chat alone and Bash gave me good advice about helping Derek, who was older and senior and an exceptionally strong personality. Derek walked with him later and came back asserting that he had converted Bash to his views; since Derek had turned against the 'simplicity' of the Christian Union and reverted to a strident religiosity, Bash must have been most tactful.

His calm handling of what to me was a major crisis, and his prayers, had their reward. On 25th July, two days before the finish of the Cricket Quarter (as it was called at Charterhouse) Derek and I had a long conversation in the study we shared. At last 'Derek's face betrayed his feelings; there was a long silence. Then he said, "Shall we end with prayer?" And by the words he used, by his voice and his face, I *knew* he had turned back to Jesus.'

Bash had invited me to stay a night at Maidenhead on my way home to Hertfordshire but this was not possible. Both Derek and I spoke to him on the telephone and I arranged to meet him in London the following Monday alone as Derek's home was in the Lake District. Over luncheon I told Bash all the news. 'I also asked him whether he thought I was wrong in being away from home so much, and he said it did not matter so long as I didn't "queer the pitch" at home. Everything – and I agree with him entirely – was to be subordinated to the great battle for HIM.' In retrospect I must say that my elderly parents, with their two older sons at the War and their daughter married, showed much generosity and patience.

Bash and I did some shopping, failed to get another potential camper to join us for tea, and ended by going to the house where I was born, which was shut up for the duration (or in fact until it was damaged in an air raid.) There among the dust sheets in the drawing-room we 'had a terrific QT and then prayed out all our needs.

I feel so strengthened after it, so joyful and thankful to the Lord Jesus – and to Bash.'

My diary dried up that August in the exhaustion of farming. After Derek and I had bicycled from the school camp near Chard to Iwerne we found we were 'in Bash's dormitory (for C.U. leaders and seconds) and the QT's are grand.' Almost nothing more appears in the diary until the last day of Camp; I was too tired to write after stooking corn or thinning plantations, while the Battle of Britain raged farther east, but I recall the way the traditional and spiritual life of Camp was cleverly dove-tailed into the demands of wartime farming and forestry, with Bash unruffled, smiling, quietly seizing opportunities for pastoral chats or teas; and never going near a stook of corn.

Bash drove me most of my way home, dropping me at Slough near Maidenhead to continue by train. I arrived at my own station to the din of the evening's Blitz and ended the journey in a lorry. That night 'the sky to the south was all lit up with a grim red glow from the great fires raging after the air raid in London.' I kept up the diary for a few days more but the strain and noise of the air raids were against it. I have never kept a journal since, except on overseas research tours.

From the many later memories of Bash that remain I will end with two. First, that of his profound help, at Iwerne in August 1942, when I heard that my next older brother, Michael, who was my dearest friend, had died of wounds in North Africa. I was eighteen and a half and at Cambridge, and had never known bereavement. Bash's handling of my grief was superb.

He had helped me to win Michael for Christ in 1940, shortly after the diary stopped. Michael and I were nearly four years apart in age but very close. His personality was specially happy and I had longed that he should know Christ as a Friend.

At that summer camp when I was first in Bash's dormitory, I asked for advice.

'Be like a dentist,' said Bash. 'You know how they probe around before doing anything. Put out a feeler, see if he is ready.'

The War had prevented much meeting but Michael and I wrote regularly. When I had returned to Charterhouse and was a little farther from the Blitz I therefore wrote proposing as a subject for discussion, 'What does it mean to be a real Christian?' Michael's reply was predictable. I then started an immense letter setting it all out, which I finished by candlelight when a distant bomb cut off our power. The letter was my first real literary attempt, which I still possess.

Michael did not reply; but his regiment was moving very soon to winter quarters near Charterhouse. Ten days later, smart in his cavalry subaltern's service dress, he took me for a walk. After a bit he said: 'You know that letter you wrote? Well, I took the step and asked him in. I agree; he makes all the difference.'

Michael had responded instantly, whereas I had struggled for weeks before accepting Christ. Michael grew fast, helped by the Officers' Christian Union; and I am sure that when Bash lay abed and my name cropped up on his prayer list, he prayed for Michael too. By the time Michael saiied for North Africa a year later he had a real Christian character and had witnessed to all his close friends and, a little shyly, to his brother-officers and his men. On the long voyage and in the Western Desert he wrote me letters which were packed with spiritual insight and encouragement as well as with his doings.

During the big battles before the fall of Tobruk in June 1942 he was hit in the head by a bomb-splinter and taken to Cairo. He was soon writing letters again. Officially he was on the danger list because, unknown to us, an internal wound would not heal; but his long and amusing letters made us assume he would recover.

It was all the more of a shock therefore on 9th August to open a grief-stricken letter from home, at breakfast in the dining room at Iwerne. I told Bash. After Prayers he took me into an empty dormitory.

'John,' he said, 'It is like having a tooth out.' (I believe Bash was having much trouble with his teeth just then.) 'It hurts like mad. But time is the healer; it really is. You don't have to worry about Michael; you know he is with the Lord and you'll meet again. But if you go around being sorry for yourself you won't be able to do your work as a Camp officer.'

I saw his point at once. Had he been sentimental I might have moped for months. Instead, a door clanged shut in my mind. Michael was in the past, the Lord was in the present. Michael was as much alive as I, and my pain looked trivial beside eternity.

In the weeks and months to come, thanks to Bash's wise handling, I was able to help my parents, carry on at Camp, and build on Michael's witness to his friends. I also told his story anonymously in an article read by officers all over the world and later put into a book.

Christ healed death's sting quickly, through Bash, and Michael's memory remains fresh after forty years. This episode was just one more in the long catalogue of Bash's pastoral ministry to me, as to hundreds of others.

The second incident is a contrast. It occurred in July 1945 when I had been in the army for two years. My deafness had stopped my going with my friends to liberate Europe. I became restless and began to agitate for a staff posting overseas since I was barred from a fighting battalion. When Bash heard of my efforts he was not sympathetic. 'You are one of the very few Camp officers still available to speak at schools,' he said. 'Your job is to stay at home and help the work.'

I thought he was wrong, and re-doubled my applications. Bash said it was pride. At last I was offered a place in South East Asia. Bash was not impressed. 'You are deserting the cause,' he said. 'What is the use of you out in Ceylon? Anybody can do it. You are needed here.' He hoped I would decline. I did not, but Bash's nagging was getting under my skin. It affected my prayer life, my peace; and at the very bottom of my mind I was hearing a still, small voice. I wrote long letters to Bash justifying my determination. He replied with a few pithy sentences which demolished my arguments.

I sensed by now that I was putting my impatience with King's Guards at St James's and recruit training before the will of God but I refused to admit it. Bash kept on at me. Then, one night, on embarkation leave with my parents, I suddenly surrendered. I knelt at my bed and asked Christ to sort out the future as he wanted. At once such extraordinary peace flooded in that it was like (in no theological sense) a second conversion.

I went overseas a different man, rediscovering the breadth and length and depth and height of Christ's love. Unknown to any of us the War was almost over and within three months I was back at Cambridge. That time abroad was to be of value to my future ministry, but it was the personal crisis beforehand, when a faithful Bash had been God's tool, that prepared me for all that followed.

Epilogue

Bash's funeral took place on a lovely spring afternoon in April, in the parish church of St Mary's, Maidenhead, where his father had for so many years been the vicar; and his ashes were later interred in the family grave.

It was a curious fact that his executors were unable to trace a single member of his family still living, and no one came forward claiming even distant relationship; and yet, as this book testifies, and the splendid crowd at his Memorial Service on June 15th, he has left behind him a host of men and women to whom he was a spiritual father; and they are linked together, not only because they regard themselves as his children in the faith, and indeed his debtors, but by their many joyful memories of a good and great man, and by the abiding eloquence of his Christian life.

Their feelings are well expressed in the words which have been inscribed on the stone at the foot of his grave: 'Remembered with love and gratitude by the many whom he led to Christ and nurtured in the Christian faith.'